TALES FROM

OUTER DARKNESS

Growing Up and Out of

the Mormon Church

by

Alan Young

TALES FROM OUTER DARKNESS

First ebook edition January 2022

First print edition March 2022

Book design by Anna Young

ISBN: 978-0-578-36832-0 (ebook)

ISBN: 978-0-578-39340-7 (paperback)

Published by Outer Darkness Press

www.alanyoungwriter.wordpress.com

Contents

Alan Young

For Charlie and Mary

TALES FROM OUTER DARKNESS

The Veil

"We must be careful that we do not destroy another person's confidence through careless words or actions."
– *Thomas S. Monson, 16th President of the Church of Jesus Christ of Latter-day Saints*

"Shall I tell you the law of God in regard to the African race? If the white man who belongs to the chosen seed mixes his blood with the seed of Cain, the penalty, under the law of God, is death on the spot. This will always be so."
- *Brigham Young, 2nd President of the Church of Jesus Christ of Latter-day Saints*

TALES FROM OUTER DARKNESS

Preface

...And It Happened Every Sunday

The blue face of my bastard alarm clock stared serenely as its ringing bell ripped me away from a wet dream, where Neve Campbell and myself were passionately necking aboard the USS Enterprise. The night before, Joe Bob Briggs had been screening *Scream* on TNT and I had been flipping between that and *Star Trek V: The Final Frontier*, so the two subjects of my affection met up and provided the scenario for my nocturnal emissions. Unfortunately, Saturday night was now a distant memory. The descending dread of Sunday morning was wrapping its legs around my neck, forcing its putrescence upon me. Bastard Sundays.

My spine curled as my mother's voice cut through the peace of the morning, splintering the wood of my bedroom door. The dread of having to get myself ready sank into my stomach and down to my feet, ensuring a slow, laborious morning process. I pushed through the fog of semi-consciousness and did my best to quiet the Brillo-Pad mop of hair that parked itself on my head. Beloved to me but a nuisance to others, my hair was long, fluffy, and as close to an Afro as a white man could naturally get. I knew that the priesthood teacher was going to hop on me for that. I could already hear his shitty voice as I tried to even out my white boy Afro:

"My, your hair is looking mightily unruly! How do you plan on getting a job looking like a hippie?"

"Well," I would reply in my coolest Bob Dylan impersonation, *"the only job I care about getting is a blow job."* At least I could be cool in my own mind. Ah, to be 14 again.

Breakfast was a luxury that time did not permit. I buttoned up my stained white dress shirt and poured myself into my incredible shrinking suit. A quick smell check told me that this was definitely the last Sunday for this suit. I tightened the knot of my Three Stooges tie and crammed my feet into my Wal-Mart loafers that had recently started to split along the sole. *Please,*

Mormon Jesus, don't let me lose my sole this Sunday. My mother loosed another shriek, signaling that the time had come to *Mach Schnell* and *Put Asses in Gear!* It was time to get a move on. After all, Mormon Jesus had a very tight schedule to keep, and he didn't need me cocking things up for everyone else.

Most mornings in Northeast Ohio are cold, wet, and gray, but somehow, it seems worse on Sundays, as if the name was some kind of sick joke. The sprinkling rain misted the windshield just enough to necessitate an occasional swipe from the ragged old wiper blades. Every minute or so, the blades hopped and skittered along the windshield, carving out a pattern of dry spots. Through the spots, I was able to gauge our distance from the church by the landmarks that we passed. The first was a crossroads, at the corner of which was a seasonal ice-cream spot. Crack Rock Johnny and I would frequent this place and try to convince the girl behind the counter that our band was *"the fucking raddest band in all the world."* I would watch as he worked over the girls, jealous that I didn't have his looks. Ah, to *not* be 14 again.

Being that this was back in a low-tech time, I would shuffle around the radio stations of the nicotine-stained Buick. Growing up, there were three big radio stations, but the only one that I bothered with was CD 93.3: THE WOLF! *That's right! Tired of shitty, overproduced pop music written by out-of-touch millionaires? The Wolf plays only the finest shitty, overproduced hard rock written by out-of-touch millionaires!* Occasionally, a good band would sneak their way into the rotation. Geddy Lee was singing about integrity in modern music as we passed the second landmark of note—the roller-rink. Luckily for me, it had not been updated since the late 70s, so it still retained its telltale brown and orange paint job and funky lettering. One night after a Young Men's and Young Women's meeting, I was asked to give a closing prayer there. I bombed so hard and was ridiculed so bad for it that I never dared pray in public again. I heard that the roller rink burned to the ground sometime last year, making it the second-worst disaster that ever happened there.

Lil' Mack's was the third landmark and was the one I had the least aversion to. It was a dumpy little bodega run by a man who wore a perpetually stained trucker hat that read, *'Don't steal from the government. They don't like the competition!'* Often, we would stop here after church so that Mom could get a carton of cigarettes and a case of beer after being told by the ward *not* to buy a carton of cigarettes and a case of beer. Sometimes the lesson doesn't land quite the way you think it will. *C'est la vie.*

With each passing landmark, I could feel the anxiety growing throughout my body. My stomach flipped at the sight of each familiar stone and mailbox. I dreaded the empty fields, the tilted garages, and the overflowing ditches because I knew that I would be pushed from my world of classic rock and dumped into the white bread world of the Warren ward. Those Sunday mornings were all the same. Get up, be miserable, get in the car, drive, get to church, be miserable. A misery sandwich.

The final landmark was the empty field next to the cemetery. The cemetery itself was unremarkable—

a typical monument to the delusion of resurrection. The empty field was far more interesting. I had always wondered if the land belonged to the cemetery owners or if someone intended to build a house there. I wouldn't mind it. Quiet neighbors. Whether living or dead, that land was sure to have tenants one day. Neil Young was singing about O-HI-O as the church came into view. My empty stomach rumbled as the anxiety washed over me. I tried to push the hunger out of my mind. The next three hours did not belong to me. They belonged to the collective. Stories of ancient peoples that never existed, with magic changing skin and plates of gold would be the stewards. It belonged to people who were so certain of their beliefs that they could not and would not entertain any notion that they might be wrong. The next three hours belonged to Jesus, Joseph Smith, and the world of make-believe...and it happened every Sunday.

Part One

Jesus Wants Me for a

Sunbeam...Or So I'm Told

"In these respects we differ from the Christian world, for our religion will not clash with or contradict the facts of science in any particular."

- Brigham Young, 2nd President of the Church of Jesus Christ of Latter-day Saints

"The first myth we need to eliminate is that 'Book of Mormon' archeology exists. If one is to study Book of Mormon archeology, then one must have a corpus of data with which to deal. We do not. The Book of Mormon is really there so one can have Book of Mormon studies, and archeology is really there so one can study archeology, but the two are not wed. At least they are not wed in reality since no Book of Mormon location is known with reference to modern topography." *- Dee F. Green, Mormon archeologist.*

14

TALES FROM OUTER DARKNESS

15

Chapter 1

I Hope They Call Me on a Mission

In my ward, there was a special wall opposite the bishop's office devoted to all the accomplishments and honors belonging to church members. Actually, let me amend that. The wall was devoted to all the accomplishments and honors that the *MEN* were responsible for. The only mention of the many great and noble deeds done by our sisters and mothers was a dusty plaque nailed underneath the light switch in the corner. I once asked why the women's plaque was situated underneath the light switch. The response I got from the bishop was, "Because women light the future."

In any case, the church was very supportive toward *those who achieved.* Why wouldn't it be? To be fair, it takes a lot of devotion, time, and effort to engage in the activities and organizations of such a high-demand religion like Mormonism. How do you expect to keep members paying tithes and giving up their free time if you don't recognize them from time to time? However, in any arena, there are winners and there are losers. I find the losers fascinating.

What of those who don't quite make it all the way to the top? What of those who by physical, cultural, or intellectual limitations can't achieve at the highest level? What happens when you try your hardest and *still* fail? Quiet failure can often suffocate an individual simply by the amount of attention put on it. It is impossible to fail in secret in the Mormon church. Secrets don't exist in the Mormon church, except in the temples. When you fail in the church, *everyone* knows about it.

The Mormon church has a culture of conspicuous achievement, though one could argue that culture applies to a lot of other religions. In the dick measuring contest of modern religion and false righteousness, our religion needs to have more meat than a Texas barbecue. Members were often obsessed with showing the world and the ward that they were doing good, that they were succeeding. Success is measurable and, therefore, validates one's actions.

Like most other Christian religions, church comes with Sunday school. In the Mormon church, the class for the school-age kids was called Primary, the idea being that what you learn in that class sets the foundation for the rest of your life in the church. I can remember singing a song as a kid in Primary called 'I Hope They Call Me on a Mission', a song dedicated to indoctrinating very young children to leave their families for two years and go spread the word of the church. To be fair, they wait till you are the ripe old age of 18 to send you away, so it's not as bad as I make it out to be. Though, when I come to think of it, 18 years is still pretty young. I mean, at 18, I was an expert at exactly two things—my penis and my alcoholism. Quite often, one would interrupt the affairs of the other. I suspect it's adorable to hear your young child sing about wanting to take on the world in a very adult way when they can't even tie their own fucking shoelaces. However, it might be nice for kids to enjoy their childhood a bit. In the end, the song is cultish, indoctrinating, and sounds an awful lot like the songs my Uncle Fritz had to sing during World War II.

The most frightening image that sticks with me, even all these years later, is that of one of my Primary classmates with a 'Future Missionary' name tag on. This little angelic steward of religious fervor strutted into Primary with his chest puffed out, and sat in the front row beaming with pride. Our Primary teacher, a weepy middle-aged woman who longed for children of her own, rushed over and swept him up into a bountifully suffocating long hug.

"Look!" she exclaimed as she turned to the rest of us. "He's got the right idea! Heavenly Father will be so lucky to have him on a mission!"

"It was a gift from my dad!" cried the little boy as he looked up at her with a stoic pride uncharacteristic of non-indoctrinated children. "I'd go tomorrow if I could, but Mom says I have homework to finish!"

The Primary teacher let out a howl of laughter and crunched him up into a hug one more time. He sat down next to me, polished his name tag, and opened his well-worn scriptures. In that moment, I think a part of me understood what just happened. I didn't feel jealous. I did not want to be him. On the contrary, I felt sorry for the kid. He was fucked. He *had* to go now. His future had been decided for him the moment his dad popped that nametag on him. Shit, if you don't stick to your mission commitment after that, I don't know what you'd do.

In any case, there I was in Primary, wearing my reflective suit that my mom bought from a guy named Tony out of the back of a truck, and singing along to the tune. As I mindlessly sang, I wondered to myself what a mission consists of. Whenever Inspector Gadget was sent on a mission, it was typically very dangerous and fraught with peril. Only with the help of his niece, Penny (who I had a thing for), and her dog, Brain, would he get out of these sticky situations and complete his mission. As I sang the final verse, I wondered if they would issue you a dog and a Penny before they send you on a mission?

As a child, I had no idea what a mission was, I just knew that I *had* to go on one. We had entire lessons on why it was imperative that all MEN go on a mission. Women were encouraged to go on a mission *only* if they weren't already married and working on their brood by the age of 18. Mission: Optional.

"The world needs you," the teacher would say. "How are we ever to rid the world of sin unless you, Brother Young, get up off your lazy little kid butt and go out and convince people to join this church that you yourself know very little about? Put down the Dunkaroos and go!" As an adult, that is a hard sell, but as a kid, you accept it because a grown-up is telling you to.

Wanting to get it over with, I resigned myself to go on a mission as a seven-year-old. I'd told my parents that I *had* to go on a mission, that our teacher was adamant that we all go. I told them with a tremor in my voice that I might not be home for a while and not to bother saving my dinner. They laughed and went back to watching Star Trek as I shuffled off to my room, trying to decide which Goosebumps books I wanted to take with me on my mission. I didn't want to go. I wanted to play and be a kid. That is a lot of heaviness to put into a child's head. Fortunately for myself, I remained a lazy cad for most of my life and never got around to going on a mission. Alcohol and glue sniffing will do that to you.

In those beige and taupe layered hallways, I would often overhear conversations between terrified mothers and the ward Gossip about different young men on their missions and how they were doing. This was at a time when missionaries could only call home TWICE a year. It's a good idea to throw innocent and unknowing 18-year-old boys into a hostile world and cut them off from their families. Builds character. The conversations would sound something like this:

> **Concerned Mother**: *Oh, did I tell you? Dallin called last night!*
>
> **Ward Gossip**: *Oh wow! How's he doing?*
>
> **Concerned Mother** (trying to fight back tears): *He's doing great! He's...he's really feeling the spirit.*
>
> **Ward Gossip**: *Oh, I don't know how you do it. Sending your boy to Central America with the condition that it's in. I heard that they were castrating people with rusty soup can tops!*

Concerned Mother: *Well, he's got the spirit of the Lord to protect him!*

Yeah, well, the "spirit" has a very low success rate against castration with rusty objects. Actually, last time I checked, God has *caused* more deaths than he's stopped. I'm pretty sure the numbers back me up on this one. However, with all that risk and heartache, it didn't stop people from subtly pressuring young men into committing two of their most formative years to being door-to-door salesmen of the wild ramblings of a film-flam artist and con-man, the notorious Joseph Smith.

One of these young men in our ward had his picture on the wall of honor for earning his Eagle Scout. We'll call him Brother Good Guy because he was honestly a good guy, always even-keeled and always looked out for us younger kids. As a kid, I got picked on a lot because I had glasses bigger than my fucking face (thank you, 1993!). This guy would always step in and stop the other kids from picking on me, fix me up, gimmie a pep talk, the whole nine yards. He liked to help those in need, so I think that a mission would have been very attractive to him.

Anyway, Brother Good Guy came of age and it was floated around that he would probably be going on his mission soon. His mother and father scraped together every single spare nickel and dime they had, even reaching out to people in the church to help with the costs. It's ironic that a church that prides itself on how much money it makes actually charges its poorest members to go out and do its dirty work. With the amount of money the church has at its disposal, it could easily send every man and woman of mission age anywhere in the world and have enough to cover rent, food, and expenses. The church's logic for hoarding its wealth is that they are saving it for the second coming of Christ, because, you know, Jesus needs that money!

As I said, he was very well-liked by everyone in the ward, so we all got together and threw him a big going away party. Brother Good Guy stood with Mother and Father Good Guy, receiving kisses from the old ladies and vigorous backslaps and handshakes from the old men. I went up and just thanked him for looking out for me and for being such a cool guy. He tousled my hair and gave me a handshake. The party peaked when the bishop and Father Good Guy *bestowed a blessing unto him*, essentially ensuring him that God was gonna watch his ass. He was a made man.

On Sunday, I'd pass the wall of honor, looking up at the proud portraits of all those conspicuously successful people, basking in their achievement as they furthered the legitimacy of the church. Even though I knew I wouldn't belong there, I still went every Sunday and waved to the picture of Brother Good Guy, wished him well, and went on to have another boring Sunday.

A few months later, my mom told me that I needed to say a prayer for Brother Good Guy. She seemed anxious and there was a foreboding in her plea for prayer. Immediately, I suspected the worst.

"He's sick? Is he hurt?" I asked with genuine concern.

"No, he's..." Mom started but didn't know how to answer. "Just pray."

So, I did. I figured it must be bad if *I* needed to pray. I mean, Brother Good Guy had been blessed by the bishop, for Chrissakes! If that wasn't enough, he surely must be in trouble. He was a good guy. I didn't want anything bad to happen.

The next Sunday, I did my usual circuit past the wall of honor to do my usual good luck wave to the portrait of Brother Good Guy. I noticed that something was drastically different. When I looked up at the wall, I could not find the portrait of Brother Good Guy anywhere. The spot where I had looked up and wished luck to so many times was bare. All that was left was a ring of dirt where his picture once hung. *Maybe it fell*, I thought as I scanned the floor. Since I couldn't find it, I assumed that it had been stolen by high-tech art bandits. Hey, it happened all the time on Inspector Gadget. It seemed like a rational explanation.

The ward Gossip spoke in hushed tones as I passed her in the hallway on the way to the morning services, but I couldn't make anything out. It sounded serious, though. I parked myself next to my mom and flipped through the hymnal when, from the corner of my eye, I saw Mother and Father Good Guy making their way in. They had forlorn looks on their faces. It was different from the looks on the faces of the parents of active missionaries. They usually had a look of pride mixed with extreme dread on their faces. Mother and Father Good Guy had a different look altogether. It was *shame!* Had something happened to Brother Good Guy?

They took their usual seats and left a space between them. The chatting of the congregation died at once as I looked up to see Brother Good Guy, his head hung low, making the long walk to the vacant space between his parents. A wave of relief came over me. Brother Good Guy was ok! I'd have to remember to give him a big hello when I could. Curiously, I noticed that no one else seemed to be as excited as I was, least of all his parents who actually looked embarrassed to be seen with him. Clearly something was going on that I wasn't privy to.

After services, I made my way to the bathroom to relax and reflect on the oddness that was going on in the ward. I locked myself in the handicapped stall and began to contemplate the vast complexities of the curious looks and unsaid phrases that grownups could understand, but were mysterious to me. In short, I was trying to figure out what the fuck all that weirdness was about. My contemplation was interrupted by the sound of the door bouncing open, followed by two loud boisterous voices doing a healthy bout of shit talking. I froze in the stall and tried to keep myself as quiet as possible as the two voices tried to out-dude each other.

> **Brother Dude #1:** *Dude, I heard he didn't even unpack his bags before he wanted to go home, dude.*

> **Brother Dude #2:** *No, dude, I heard that he froze up on his first call, dude. He got there and he didn't know anything about the Book of Mormon. He just stuttered like a weenie!*

> **Brother Dude #1:** *Dude, can you believe that he showed up today? Man, I wouldn't show my face after bailing out of a mission, dude!*

> **Brother Dude #2:** *Dude, I know, dude! I'd rather die than come back early!*

As they tumbled out into the hallway, I mulled over their dude-laden conversation. *That was it? He came home early? That's all?* Brother Good Guy had done so much for these two little shits and here they were, talking about him like he was a punk. Was it possible that all of his good deeds were, in fact, so fragile that they were erased with this single event? It seemed that the opinion of the dudes was echoed through the rest of the ward. Little sly conversations in code and sideways glances at Brother Good Guy told the story. Opinions and condemnations spoken with eyes. Churches are like echo chambers; the emotional noise builds on itself until you can't hear anything else.

After classes, I scoured the hallway looking for Brother Good Guy, hoping to tell him that no matter what, I still respected him. I looked all around, but I couldn't find him. I wasn't even able to find Father and Mother Good Guy. As time went on, we saw less and less of the Good Guy family at church. When they stopped showing up completely, I don't remember anyone bothering to ask about them. I'm still not entirely sure what happened to him on his mission that cut it so short. Maybe he got homesick, something so natural and understandable for an 18-year-old? Maybe he saw something on his mission that fucked him up? After all, not everyone gets sent to Orlando.

Maybe he had doubts about the church? After all, when you are cloistered with a bunch of other scared kids away from home for the first time, facing resistance of your message every day from a cold and angry world, it either strengthens your faith or breaks it. Maybe he wasn't drinking the Kool-Aid anymore. This is the one that I think about often. I'll never know for sure. What I do know is that, from the moment he came home early, he was *dead. Persona non grata. A punk.* His past accomplishments, even his character was worthless because of his inability to finish his mission. Anything less than total success is total failure. There is no middle ground in the church. All that respect and love was gone. All that was left was a dirty ring on a wall where his picture once was.

Chapter 2

Have Yourself a Shitty Little Christmas

In continuing with this perverse recollection of my time in the Mormon church, I find myself once again thinking of Christmases of yesteryear. Fond memories of opening presents on a snowy Christmas morn, stuffing my fat face with lebkuchen that Oma had made the night before, and getting yelled at by my parents to hurry up and make the coffee, swim in the pools of nostalgia in my mind. Christmases were hit or miss for me. I had no 'normal' Christmases as it were. Then again, I don't know of *any* family whose definition of normal matched up with one another. Let's just say that, for me, some years were less weird than others. Other years appeared to be lost episodes from the Twilight Zone. *This* particular story is of the latter.

One morning in early December, our Bishop announced to the ward that there would be a Christmas celebration unlike anything there had ever been. He looked out at the bleary eyes of the adults and the wandering ones of the children, scanning for any sign of excitement. He must have thought that this announcement would really get people amped and juiced up with the Christmas spirit. It didn't. Such is life. The women-folk did their best to get the men-folk to sit up straight and pay attention. Good luck, Sister Wonderbread. Your hubby has got the Browns game on his mind.

In my attempt to stave off the boredom, I was busy sliding my forehead along the fabric of the chair next to me, slowly wearing a hole into my skin. As a kid, this repeated action made complete sense to me. If you're bored, run your forehead across the fabric of the chair. It's instant fun! Unfortunately, I was not aware of the consequences of such fun. The open wound that it produced would burn horrifically for the next three days, but for the moment, it assuaged my boredom. Eh, what did I know? I was ten.

"Yes, everyone, we are going to take a time machine back to the very first Christmas!" proclaimed the bishop in an attention-grabbing baritone. The congregation snapped to attention. I lifted my reddened forehead to see if he was for real. *Did he do it? Has he figured out time travel?* My wide eyes were glued, waiting for Doc and Marty to show up. Maybe he would let me borrow the time machine. I'd always wanted to see a dinosaur. Shit, I always wanted to *ride* a dinosaur! Christmas in Jurassic Park? This would be the best Christmas ever!

Alas, our Bishop did not have a time machine, nor did he even have a DeLorean. That cracker drove a Bronco. What he did have was a plan to transform the entire church into a Bethlehem marketplace, equipped with places to buy "traditional" bread, clothes, fruits, and anything else you could imagine. We would be able to "actually experience what it was like when Christ was born into this world," and if that weren't epic enough, there would be a recreation of the nativity. That's right! Baby Jesus was gonna worm his way out of the Virgin Mother in a special one-time-only performance! *Get your tickets now!* Now, nativity plays are nothing new. But, let's think about the practice for a moment, shall we? The congregation (which is mostly people of the Caucasian persuasion), is pretending to be middle-eastern people, celebrating the birth of a child who will one day be betrayed, tortured, killed, and resurrected, only to have his message distorted and his death glorified. Does that sound weird to *anyone* else, or is it just me?

The congregation looked on with uncertainty. Other wards had pulled this kind of thing off, but not ours. It would require a lot of work that nobody wanted to do in order to pull this off. Luckily for us, the bishop had a solution.

"Throughout the day, I will call certain individuals to volunteer for tasks I feel they would be right for. This will help us ensure that everyone takes part and pride in this most joyous celebration of Christ." The Mormon church prides itself on having no professional clergy. Theoretically, any person that devotes enough time to the church could be placed in charge of Sunday school classes or in charge of running the ward, regardless of qualifications. What that means is that, at some point, you might be called on to devote a significant portion of your free time to do work (for free) for the church. Now, you add on special events like the one our Bishop just sprang on us, you start to see how much time the church demands of its members. Sometimes, there just aren't enough hours in a week. If there is one thing the church does better than anyone, it is involuntary volunteerism.

Being that I was a kid, I hadn't expected to get assigned to anything. Most ten-year-olds like me were grossly incompetent at anything worthwhile. My world consisted of Goosebumps books, Jurassic Park, and watching monster movies, and I was in no way qualified enough to help *put on a show*! So, you can imagine my surprise when the bishop pulled me out of class and into his office.

"Brother Young, I have a very important task for you to complete. You are going to be our banker!" The bishop sat back in his chair and looked upon me as if I'd been tapped for greatness, waiting to see me gush with gratitude.

"Um, like in Monopoly?" I asked timidly as my chubby little legs dangled off of the edge of the chair. "I'm not too good with math yet. Can I at least have a calculator?"

"No calculators," he said confidently. "Remember, this is Bethlehem of the *past*. Don't worry about math. Heavenly Father has told me that you are going to be a great mathematician someday and this is your chance for greatness. What do you think of that?"

"I think Heavenly Father would want me to have a calculator," I said.

The bishop waved me off. "Now, you are going to have to get some gold."

"Gold?" I asked.

"Yes! In biblical times, they didn't have coins like we do now!" *Yeah, if those Romans lacked one thing, it was coins.* "Do you know how to make gold?"

I racked my ten-year-old brain and then landed on my answer. "I could find a leprechaun! Or rob a bank! Or find a genie like Aladdin." Of the options, robbing a bank seemed least practical, once again because I was ten.

"Look," groaned the bishop. "You just gotta spray paint some rocks gold. Make ten pieces per pouch and give every family one pouch. If they want more, they have to buy more. Can you handle that?"

"I..."

"Great!" snapped the bishop. "Ok, back to class! See you in a few days!"

I was hurried into the hallway—another victim of involuntary volunteerism. *Heavenly Father thinks I'm good at math? Is he out of his mind?* I hated math. Math and I did not get along. I wanted to beat the shit out of math. Surely a just and loving God *knew* that I hated math. If he did, why would he tell the bishop to give me this titanic task? Does God like to fuck with ten-year-old boys, or is that just his clergy? In either case, I was going to have to do something that I absolutely did not want to do. The hole that I had worn into my forehead kept stinging me all day. Mom had tried her best to clean it with antiseptic, but my agonized screams and protestations created a substantial barrier to her success. I would have to suffer for my idiocy. I would also have to suffer for the Christmas vision of the bishop.

On the way home from church, we had stopped by Stambaugh's Hardware in Warren, the last refuge for mean old salty bastards to buy nail-guns and talk shit about their wives. Luckily for me, there were enough of them mulling about in the aisles to help me find a can of gold spray paint to create bootleg gold for the merry Mormon masses. They were less curious as to why a child needed a can of spray paint, and more curious as to why I had a giant patch of missing skin from my forehead.

"What in the hell happened to you, boy? You get a half-ass scalpin' from an Indian or somethin'?" asked a surly old man who had a face like an old baseball glove. *No, your daughter got too excited and wouldn't let me come up for air.* I paid for the spray paint with a crumpled five and left the old men to commiserate about the loss the Browns just suffered.

Back at home, I asked my mom if she would help me spray paint the rocks. Sensing that this would be a perfect opportunity for her dear son to learn a useful skill, she showed me the basics of spray painting and left me to my own devices. The only specific instruction she gave me was to "Do that outside, or in the garage!"

Since there was two feet of snow on the ground, I headed out into the garage. I laid the rocks out on the bare floor and debated my next move. I supposed that all I had to do was to press the nozzle down. Mom had gone so fast with the tutorial that all I caught was the lecture about how pissed my dad would be if I got spray paint on the garage floor. *No matter*, I thought, *I'll just aim really careful with the nozzle. I got good aim!* I stood over the rocks, pointed the can at them, and pressed the nozzle. A jet of gold mist erupted from the nozzle and coated the raw skin of my forehead. The goddamn nozzle was pointed in the wrong direction. A searing, burning pain emanated from my forehead. Apparently, spray paint on raw skin serves as an irritant. I would have to deal with it later. I pointed the nozzle the right way toward the rocks and let it rip. The rocks absorbed the gold spray paint, as well as the concrete floor, my dad's tools that lined the walls, my winter jacket, and my lungs. Turns out that my aim was *not* so good. I had also neglected to open any windows or doors, so I was treated to a very nasty spray paint high. As a teenager, I would grow to appreciate inhalants, but only in a limited capacity. I stumbled inside the house, gilded forehead and all, presented my mother with the can of spray paint, and passed out in the hallway.

The next night was the Christmas shindig. I watched with curiosity as Mom tossed a pile of tablecloths and masking tape down on the floor in front of me.

"What's that?" I asked, understandably curious. The last time I had seen a pile of sheets and a roll of tape was at the beginning of a horror movie.

"Those are our costumes," Mom said.

I observed the paisley printed tablecloth with the pasta stain and wondered how exactly this fit in with the birth of Christ. Did Jesus have pasta for his first meal? Was Jesus Italian? Was that why the Catholic Church was big in Rome? My head swam with these theological questions while I watched my mom go to work. She picked up the paisley printed tablecloth with the pasta stain, tossed it over my head, and folded it in half so that I could see. The coarse fabric felt like sandpaper over my raw, spray-painted forehead. She grabbed the masking tape, and with five quick, precise swipes, taped a headband around the tablecloth, and thus completed my 'Bethlehem' costume. Looking back, I am glad that no picture exists of this (that I know of). I looked like a bad guy from the Naked Gun movies. Mom completed her own costume and then turned to my dad. He was busy attempting to wipe the gold spray paint off his socket wrench.

"You ready for your costume?" asked Mom. She had somehow convinced him to take time out of his car repairing and home improvement to come to Church.

"Nope," said Dad.

"Everyone is doing it," she pressed. "You'll look stupid if you are the only one without a costume on," said Mom.

Dad eyed me as I tried desperately to relieve the pressure from the masking tape around my head, turned back to Mom, and laughed out loud. "Shit!" he said, shaking his head. It is at this point I wish to take a moment to talk about my dad. He is not a loquacious man. In fact, I am convinced that, in my dad's whole life, he's only ever needed three words—yep, nope, and shit. In any given instance, my dad's reaction would be accompanied by one of these words. For example:

Me: Hey, Dad, the basement flooded again.

Dad: Yep.

Me: That's not gonna be very good for the foundation.

Dad: Nope.

Me: Oh, man, I think the septic tank is leaking!

Dad: Shit!

Christmas was particularly fun to watch to see how Dad would react.

Me: Good lot of presents this year.

Dad: Yep.

Me: I bet this reminds you of Christmases back when you were a kid, right, Dad?

Dad: Nope.

Me: Really? What were they like?

Dad: Shit.

I envied my dad that night. I would have given anything to get that tablecloth off my head. I could feel it grafting itself to my forehead through the sweat and plasma that was leaking out of my wound. However, I would have to wait till later to rip it off my skin. I was on my way to attend to the fiduciary needs of the Warren ward. I piled all the rocks that I had spray-painted into a grocery bag and chucked it in the back of our van. Dad looked over the gold paint on the floor of the garage, shook his head sadly, and hopped in the front seat. I've never seen my father get more depressed than when something happens to his garage. Right now, he was on suicide watch, courtesy of my little stunt with the spray can. We would both have to wait to wallow in our misery. We were off into the frozen night.

****

Upon arriving at the church, we were greeted by the sight of our Bishop, anxiously pacing in the parking lot in full Bethlehem regalia. He was also dressed like a Naked Gun villain; a hodgepodge of middle-eastern and old testament stereotypes. On top of his head sat a turban, under which his face was painted light brown. His fake beard reached down to his navel, gently tucked into his sash that held up his prop sword. I stared at this cultural atrocity pacing around in the Northeast Ohio snow, wondering what the hell we were getting into. As my dad stubbed out his cigarette, I could hear him mutter something that sounded distinctly like "shit".

I dragged my bag of spray-painted rocks across the slush that layered the parking lot and into the church. The bishop eagerly dug through the bag, looked upon my handiwork, and groaned.

"Brother Young, what is this?" he asked with dark authority.

"Gold?" I replied. He looked over the contents sternly and picked up one of the specimens.

"The paint hasn't even dried! What am I supposed to do?" he groaned. *I don't know, maybe don't entrust the financial stability of a fake Bethlehem to a ten-year-old?* He waved us away and started dabbing the excess paint off the rocks. My feeling of self-worth was pretty low at this point. That's alright, it prepared me for how I would feel for most of my childhood.

We made our way into the chapel where we were greeted with a hodgepodge of set decorations of various quality. There was a bakery facade that looked quite well done. Whoever made it had painted it to look like it was made from palm leaves and other stuff you might find in the desert. Next to that was a cardboard storefront that was supposed to belong to a snake charmer. The guy behind the cardboard façade was wearing a bath towel wrapped around his head, also painted brown, also with a sword. I looked around and I noticed that almost everyone had swords. Come to think of it, this was right around the time *Aladdin* came out, so I suppose that explains why everyone had swords. Anyway, at his feet was a wicker basket with a rubber snake hanging out of the side. I observed the prop with polite intrigue.

"CAREFUL, MY FRIEND! I MIGHT BE A SNAKE CHARMER, BUT THIS LITTLE FELLA LOOKS HUNGRY!" he boomed at me as I passed with trepidation. He then performed an extended ululation that rang out through the church, eliciting laughs from some of the older members. *"Oh, he's like that fella on the Simpsons! Thank you, come again!"*

I did my best to keep close to my family. The bishop had apparently given up on my spray-painted rocks. I watched as people exchanged good ol' American money for pieces of pita bread at one of the stands. My heart sunk because I felt that not only did I disappoint the bishop, but I also disappointed God. It would not be the last time. In any case, the night was moving on to the main event—the birth of Christ. The bishop may have miscast his ten-year-old banker, but he was certain to get the right people to play the Christ family. For the task, he tapped an entire family that was more than happy to represent the Christs. They were the picture-postcard walking stereotypes of a Mormon family, with 15 children (none of which liked me) and seats on the stake presidency.

They were and are nice people, but I always sensed that it made my parents uneasy. How can you compete with people like that? I always saw my dad especially get quiet around them. Once, in an uncharacteristic outpouring of words, I heard him remark, "I've never seen them get angry. I wonder if they even know how." For the purposes of this story, we'll call them Brother and Sister Mooreman and The Brood. The Mooremans took their marks in the manger set. The lights dimmed dramatically. The bishop looked on, chewing his nails down to the cuticles. Child #8 from the Mooreman Brood stepped forward and opened the scene for the eager audience.

"Ladies and gentlemen, I bring you to Bethlehem! The year: zero!" There was polite laughter. "The day: well...CHRISTMAS!" The audience burst into applause. My dad rolled his eyes so far into the back of his head, I am certain that he could see his goddamn brain stem.

Brother and Sister Mooreman acted as a less-than-visibly pregnant Mary and a very visibly portly Joseph. Brother Mooreman stepped forward with a toothy Mormon smile and proclaimed "Glory to this night! For we, the people of Earth, are about to receive a gift from the planet Kolob!" Some of the newer converts looked around to the more experienced of us and asked what Kolob was. *Sister Sarah, if you gotta ask, you don't wanna know.*

Sister Mooreman lay on a bed of straw. Brood members #5, #6, and #7 served as the Three Wise Men. The rest of the Brood served as various shepherds and anxious onlookers, all of them with the same vapid, empty smiles on their faces. There was a murmur of affection throughout the crowd.

"That woman must have tent flaps by now!" Mom muttered as she counted the Mooreman brood under her breath. It's only now that I realize what she meant by that.

"Hark!" shouted Brood member #2, "I think I hear the Christ approaching!" It was at this moment that Sister Mooreman, no stranger to *actual* childbirth, let loose a very real, very graphic torrent of pregnancy screams. She clenched her fists around the straw that littered the scene and began flailing violently, showering the first few rows with debris. The audience watched in horror as the "miracle" of childbirth was brought to life. It was method acting at its finest. Robert De Niro couldn't even touch it. It was at this moment that the blanket covering the bottom part of Sister Mooreman started to wriggle in horrific and unnatural ways. It bulged and contorted beyond the shape of any pregnancy that has ever taken place on the planet Earth. I was reminded of the chest-burster scene in *Alien*, only, instead of a little baby alien, there was a little baby Mormon ripping through the guts of a screaming, writhing woman.

A tiny human arm emerged from underneath the blanket. A sharp giggling could be heard from what passed as her pregnant belly. Even as a ten-year-old, I was fairly certain that babies didn't make sounds while still inside the mother, and yet the giggling became louder and more intense. Brother Mooreman popped his head underneath the blanket and reached both his arms in.

"Behold! The Christ Child!" he exclaimed as he pulled a gigantic baby out by its chubby arm. The child was Brood member #15, a husky one-year-old who was now chewing on the straw in his hand like he was Old McDonald. The little one pulled off the fake beard and kicked at the sword on Brother Mooreman's hip as he attempted to bless the child. He held the squirming, straw-covered child aloft as his Brood joined in an impromptu chorus of 'Hosanna!'

The audience split between those who were horrified and those who were humbled. The bishop did his best to get us to join in the 'Hosanna' that was happening to mixed results. The old guys in the ward sang out of tune with gusto while munching on pita. The husky baby Jesus was now slapping Joseph on his cheeks, trying desperately to get to his mother for milk. The bishop's time-traveling experiment to ancient Bethlehem had gone awry. Never again would our ward attempt anything so grand. A feeling of relief flooded over me as I watched the baby Jesus now grab his father's sword and stuff it into the back of his father's knees. I was relieved that my little mishap with the rocks would be ultimately forgotten.

It was at this moment that my dad decided to step out and get away from the farce that was happening in the chapel. I made my way outside with him. He popped a cigarette in his mouth, took a drag, and shook his head.

"That was…pretty weird, Dad," I said as I kicked a mound of snow off the sidewalk.

"Yep," he replied with deep terror. "Yep, yep, yep."

"Is that what having a baby is really like?" I imagined what my own birth must have been like. Did I also crawl out of my mother and start slapping my father in the face? Are babies *that* rude?

"Yep," he replied, the same terror in his voice. *Note to self: never have kids!*

I looked out at the night, watching my dad finish his cigarette. I knew that we weren't supposed to smoke or drink booze or coffee, but my parents did all of that. Even though the church was against it, I couldn't be against it because my parents did it. I loved them too much. In the choice between church and family, family wins every time. For once, I think my parents were glad they weren't like the Mooremans. We may not have been very good at being Mormon, but at least we were honest about it. There were no vapid smiles, no happy proclamations of Jesus coming down from another planet, and no pressure to be perfect. For that moment, we were united in imperfection. I appreciated that.

My dad looked down at me and smiled at my little costume. I had forgotten all about it while inside, but I started to notice the itchiness of the tablecloth against my raw forehead. It was time to take it off.

"Dad, could you help me get this thing off my head?"

"Yep," he said. He parked his cigarette between his lips and started unwrapping the masking tape. I could feel the pressure releasing and my brain finally ingesting the glorious oxygen it craved. I went to pull it off the rest of the way, but to my horror, I found that it was not budging. I tugged and tugged, but all I felt was pain. It was then I realized that the tablecloth had fused to the wound on my forehead.

"Dad, it's stuck! What do I do?" I cried frantically. Terrible thoughts of having to go through life with a tablecloth stuck to my head played out in my mind. Would I have to pretend to be a man from Bethlehem to make my life less miserable? It was ok at Christmastime, but during the Fourth of July, I was sure to get my ass kicked. This was Ohio, after all. They only like middle-eastern people at Christmas and not so much any other time.

"Hold on," said my dad in a reassuring voice as he grasped the corner of the tablecloth. "Ready?"

"Ready for what?" Fast tearing sounds followed by a torrent of swear words echoed through the parking lot. I clenched my forehead in pain, the flesh burning where the tablecloth used to be. I can still hear my dad's booming laughter echoing through the cold December night.

Chapter 3

That One Time the Three Stooges Ruined Church

Before I start this next section, it should be noted that I don't believe in a god, miracles, the supernatural, the zodiac, or other mystical forces in the universe. I don't believe in second or third lives and I don't really believe that anything happens for a reason. I think that we as humans tend to seek order in the chaos that is life. With that being said, sometimes that chaos provides some much-needed flavor to a dull morning.

By the time I was 12, I was making my way through the church at a glacial speed. I didn't excel in any of my Sunday school classes, I hadn't read the Book of Mormon or the Bible for that matter. With the exception of the Scouts, I showed little signs of life concerning my celestial well-being. Sundays were no-fun-days. It was a bad way to end a week. Especially because of what happened on Saturdays...

Late-night Saturdays was where two of my favorite programs lived. I say programs because, well, I'm an old man. First, the wonderful *Monster-Vision with Joe Bob Briggs* was responsible for steadily introducing me to the movies of Wes Craven and John Carpenter, filling my head with creatures and horrors and all sorts of wonderful images. It was here that Neve Campbell and Adrienne Barbeau battled horrors that were unfathomable to those unimaginative folks at church. It was here I learned that the real monsters were the ideas behind the monsters.

Then, after that, the *Three Stooges* would come on. My mom often told me that she learned how to speak English by watching the Three Stooges, which might be the most American thing I've ever heard. Anyway, it was in the company of the Stooges where I learned how to handle most of my interpersonal conflict and create inventive solutions to simple problems. To this day, I believe that most disagreements and workplace disputes can be solved by a frying pan to the head, a 2-for-1 smack, or by simply jamming your fingers into someone's eyes. Needless to say, my work record is a little spotty, but at least I know how to do the Curly Shuffle.

One Sunday, I was actually excited to go to church. Knowing our shared love of the Three Stooges, my mother had gotten me a watch that had the Stooges on the face of it. Curly would watch the hands going around, while Moe and Larry looked on disapprovingly. The coolest thing about it was that there was this little button on the side that made the watch play 'Three Blind Mice' whenever you pushed it. Problem was that it was so big, it would routinely get caught on my pocket when I was reaching for something and go off when I didn't want it to. I had gotten in trouble for it at school when it went off in the middle of reading *Great Expectations*. Apparently, the teacher did not appreciate 'Three Blind Mice' being the soundtrack to the sorrows of Miss Havisham, that wicked old bitch.

So, there I was, sitting next to Mom in church, listening to the newest converts giving their testimony of why they *knew* the church *had* to be true and that there was no way there could ever be any question about it. Their proof was because they *felt* it to be true. As my mind drifted away from this foolproof methodology that was being paraded before me, I looked down at my watch for inspiration. Larry, Curly, and Moe looked up at me with those wonderful expressions on their faces and I enjoyed an inward giggle, thinking about the episode the night before and how I would love to poke my bishop in the eye and do the Curly Shuffle in the aisle and *nyuk nyuk nuyk* myself out the door. I *knew* that the Stooges *had* to be the funniest guys ever and there was no way there could ever be any question about it. The proof was because I *felt* it to be true. Amen.

I snapped back into reality and noticed that the congregation was starting to grow silent. That could only mean one thing—sacrament was on its way! Sacrament was always my favorite part of church. I had come to think of it as sort of a mandatory snack-time built into the service. In fact, my mother would refrain from handing me snacks during service and actually say, "You're going to eat in a second. Just hold off for a bit." Unfortunately, the body of Christ was never as filling as a granola bar, but I appreciated the gesture. Perhaps it was the fact that instead of wafers and wine, Mormons use water and white bread. You can't get too full on bread and water. Just ask any of those old-timey prisoners in those classic movies.

Before we could begin the process of chowing down on our Lord and Savior, the water and bread had to be blessed and given the holy seal of approval. Parents were hushing their children, wives were hushing their husbands, and I was trying to hush my desperately gurgling stomach. The church became deadly silent and we all waited for the blessing to start. It was the kind of quiet where you get self-conscious and actually start to think about all the physical sensations that you are feeling. Well, at this particular moment of silence in anticipation of snack time, I found myself thinking about my dry, chapped, cracked lips. I had a bad habit of licking my lips till they were so red and ragged that I looked like a cross between a crackhead and a clown. *Ronald McCrackhead.* There was only one solution was for me—Chappy Time Lip Balm! *The lip balm that keeps your lips from looking like a chapped asshole!*

I sat upright a little more, a better position for rifling around in one's pockets for their quarry. Up at the altar, the man responsible for the blessing sacrament was assuming the position for ultimate blessing power. I popped my left hand into my pocket, shuffling around for my stick of Chappy Time Lip Balm.

The young man began his prayer. "Oh, God, the eternal father, we ask thee in the name of thy Son, Jesus Christ, that you bless and sanctify this bread…"

Where was that damn lip balm? I thrust my hand in further. The watch skirted along the seam of my pocket.

"…that they may witness unto thee, oh God, the eternal father…"

My finger grazed the tube. *I can reach it if I just…*

THREE BLIND MICE! THREE BLIND MICE! SEE HOW THEY RUN! SEE HOW THEY RUN!

The childlike tune erupted from my wristwatch somewhere before the "Amen". The whole congregation stopped their prayer, popped their heads up, and turned to face me. I had 200 eyes boring into my soul, shocked and offended that, at this most sacred of moments, I would dare disturb it with such insolence! The bishop looked at me as if he were sizing me up for a coffin. Not only could I not be counted on to spray paint a bag of rocks, but I also could not be counted on to be quiet during the sacrament. I sat in ultimate cringe, feeling the fires of embarrassment and shame licking my insides. I closed my eyes, thinking that if I couldn't see them, they might not be able to see me. The tune finally subsided with all the fanfare that a wristwatch can muster and the man finished with an "Amen." The congregation mimicked and we ate our bread.

I was so mortified that I still hadn't gotten my Chappy Time out of my pocket. *I'll just have to suffer through! Like Jesus!* The Passion of the Alan had begun. I attempted to dislodge the host that was stuck to the roof of my mouth in silence, suffering right along with JC. At least I was about to get something to wash it down with because next was the water.

"Oh, God, the eternal father, we ask thee in the name of thy Son, Jesus Christ, to bless and sanctify this water, to the souls of all those who drink of it…"

My lips are burning! Maybe this is what hell is? Having chapped lips and no means to moisturize them.

"…that they may witness unto thee, oh God, the eternal father…"

That might not be a bad advertising theme. Suffering the pains of hell and nothing will quench the fire? Try new medicated *Chappy Time! Man, I really can't stand this burning! I'm not like Jesus! I'm weak!* My body had reached its limit. *IT'S CHAPPY TIME!* I recklessly plunged my hand into my pocket, ignorant of the most recent consequences. The tune burst forth in glorious irreverence.

THREE BLIND MICE! THREE BLIND MICE! SEE HOW THEY RUN! SEE HOW THEY RUN!

Once again, 200 eyes snapped my way and shot daggers aplenty as they watched me slather on the Chappy Time Lip Balm across my crusty lips. Groans of anger rippled through the congregation. Hey, fuck 'em! If they only knew the pain that I was suffering and the ecstatic relief that I was feeling, they wouldn't be so judgmental. *Besides, the song is almost over, it's ending right after this last verse.*

Only the song seemed to be starting again, not ending.

THREE BLIND MICE! THREE BLIND MICE!

Panic set in. I clapped my hand over my wrist, trying to stifle the jaunty tune. The bishop peered down at me from behind the pulpit and gave me a grave headshake of disapproval. How were we ever to get our drink of water and complete snack time if my GODDAMN WATCH WOULDN'T SHUT THE HELL UP? I frantically tried to press the button to shut it off. No good. I hoped it would stop after this next round. It didn't! IT KEPT GODDAMN GOING! A dreadful realization chilled me. *MY GODDAMN WATCH IS BROKEN!*

My mother, my poor mother, mortified by the ridiculous scene being caused by my watch with my three heroes on it, helped me out into the hallway and into the parking lot where I tossed my watch into the back seat to play out its jaunty tune for however long it saw fit. It was clearly no longer up to me. This was between Curly and God. The rest of the day was a blur of angry faces and grumblings from our dear missionaries. At some point, I prayed that I might be lucky enough to have a heart attack and maybe get to go home early, but apparently, God is selective about how he helps people. What a goon.

Three *long* hours later, when church was all over, we *finally* made our way back out to the car. I could hear the watch clear as day, still beeping away its tune and serving as a soundtrack for our trip home. The weird thing is that the watch had never gotten stuck until that day. I can only assume that the spirits of Larry Fine and Moe and Curly Howard saw how miserable I was at church and decided that divine intervention was necessary for me to survive that particular Sunday. That's the best explanation I have for it. Well, maybe the watch was manufactured with a faulty button, but this is *my* story, damnit! *I* say that the spirit of those three Jewish comedians decided to play a prank on a church full of Mormons! Funnily enough, the watch never played 'Three Blind Mice' ever again, but it still held my attention for all those dreadful Sundays when I needed it. It was a gift, from both my mother and the Three Stooges.

Chapter 4

I Can't...I'm Mormon

What is truly wonderful, even now as an Ex-Mormon, is how little people actually know about the church. It's wonderful! If you have no moral compass like me, you can exploit the ignorance of others to your advantage! I've gotten so many days off from work simply by making up a Mormon holiday and calling off. Nobody wants to fuck with that. Try it! What's the worst that could happen? You get fired? Did you really want that job anyway? Hell no, you wanna drink beer and watch *Road House* for the tenth time in a row! You got shit to do and you don't need some dumbass job getting in the way of your goals!

There were a lot of things that I wasn't supposed to do as a kid because the Mormon Church had blackballed them. I knew about the coffee ban, the tobacco ban, and the alcohol ban, but I didn't know the reasoning behind it. Legend has it that Emma Smith, the first (but not only) wife of Joseph Smith, complained about the smoking and drinking at one of the meetings. Joseph then had a 'revelation' that smoking and drinking were not groovy practices. Furthermore, he stated that coffee and tea were also not groovy, so he banned them too. You know something, it's really convenient that God gave Joseph a revelation about smoking and drinking after Emma complained. It's almost as convenient as God revealing that he wanted Joseph to practice polygamy after he had started having an affair with Fanny Alger, but that's another story. To be honest with you, I have read the Word of Wisdom and I still don't understand the coffee ban. I can understand if it's about caffeine, but then why is it ok for kids to drink energy drinks? Can we call up God and get a ruling on that?

One of my Sunday school teachers tried to explain it in Primary. She read the Word of Wisdom and tried to break it down, but we all got hung up on the "no hot drinks" section. Now, as a kid, I loved me some hot chocolate. It was one of the cornerstones of an Ohio winter. You go sledding with the gang, Oma makes you some hot chocolate, and you feel all warm and fuzzy. But now, with no hot drinks being allowed, I had to turn Oma down. *Oma, ich kann keine heise Schokolade trinken.* Sorry, Grandma, no hot chocolate for me. The prophet said so.

Oma would grimace the way that only old German women could and say, "I did not survive the allied bombings, fight off raping Russians, and tunnel under the Berlin Wall so that *meine Engel* would be stopped by some prophet!" I felt awful, mainly because I knew she was making up the part about tunneling under the Berlin Wall. Still, I guess this was to be the end of my love affair with the tiny marshmallows and the Swiss Miss. Luckily for me, my Oma had a word with the bishop and I got a special dispensation to drink my hot chocolate. *Danke, Oma.*

Anyway, I've had a few opportunities to use the church to take advantage of people. In fairness, the things that I've done were all pretty benign and I've made amends to the people wherever possible, but it's still not the coolest thing that I've ever done. Being young and stupid is a disease that we all contract at some point. The cure is when we learn from our mistakes. *If only VD were as easy!* In the spirit of honesty, I am gonna talk about them.

This little experiment started back in the fifth grade, shortly after a home visit from two of the sister missionaries. Though I was seated securely in pre-adolescence, I was still very much smitten with them, so much so that I pretty much waited on them hand and foot every time they stopped by. In one of my idiotic attempts to impress them, I had decided to try something that I had seen in a movie on *MonsterVision*. There was a slasher movie where one of the unlucky teens had frosted some glasses for beer. Apparently, this impressed his girlfriend as she replied with a cartoonish, "Classy!" Later in the film, they were beheaded with a 'dead end' road sign. Man, I love shitty jokes in shitty movies! Anyway, I knew that the sister missionaries stopped by on Tuesdays, so when I got home from school, I put a couple of glasses in the freezer to chill. When the sister missionaries stopped by, I would be able to serve them some ice-cold refreshing Coke in frosted glasses and be *the man*! Hopefully, we would not be beheaded by a clumsy pun.

The sister missionaries popped in like usual and I switched to the *Mack* mode. I grabbed their coats, tossed them in my parent's room, flashed them a quick suggestive wink, and set to work in the kitchen. I washed my hands off and, in my excitement, forgot to dry them. I then grabbed two cans of Coke from the fridge and reached up into the freezer and grabbed for the frosted glasses. As the chilled fog rolled out of the freezer, I played out the scene in brilliant full color…

I would swagger gracefully across the nicotine stained carpet, sporting two cans of Coke and two chilled glasses. The sister missionaries would be intrigued as to why such a setup was necessary for the enjoyment of their beverages. I would wow them with a careless, yet amazing flip of the cans in midair. I would crack open each can with a half-smile, winking at both of them simultaneously, maybe eliciting a slight girlish giggle from each. Softly in the background you would be able to make out the smooth sounds of Barry White. *Aww yeah!* The fizzing black beverage would flow from the cold confines of the aluminum cans into the smooth, frosted sheath of the glasses. I would give them their glasses, smile, and make my way back to my room. The entirety of the evening would be spent listening to the Sisters talking about how much of a badass, smooth, James Bond kinda fifth-grader I was. What a scene! *The Mack has attacked and all the ladies love Big Daddy A-Man!* As you might guess, things often played out better in my head than in reality.

The frosted glasses—the two vessels for my elegant showcase—were frosted all right. In fact, they were so frosted that they immediately froze themselves to my un-dried, freshly washed hands. The harder I tried to pry them apart, the more I could feel the molecules in the glass fuse with the molecules in my skin. I waved my hands frantically, trying to unstick the frosted glasses, but all that happened was the gentle tearing of my flesh. I rushed over to the sink, my hands throbbing with pain and cold, looking for a solution to this most ridiculous of problems.

Like any reasonably intelligent person, I understood that cold surfaces would often heat up when warm water was applied to them. So, I hooked one of the glasses around the hot water handle and clicked it on. I let it run for a second, ensuring the warmth of the water. It was warm, all right. In fact, it was so warm that the moment that I shoved my frozen hands under the steaming hot water, both glasses shattered and gouged deep cuts in the tips of six out of ten of my fingers. I responded with a barrage of bastardized American curse words that I had learned from my Oma. Though I knew not what they meant, I supposed the context in which they were loosed would be appropriate. As I stood watching the blood ooze between the shattered glasses, I wondered if James Bond ever had a learning curve this steep?

I eventually made my way into the living room, a canary yellow dishcloth wrapped around my mangled and bloody hands, carrying both cans of Coke underneath my armpits. The sister missionaries looked up with confusion and concern on their angelically simple faces. They observed the canary yellow dishrag that was starting to look like it had just been hunting with Dick Cheney (lol), and then looked toward the cans of Coke nestled in my pre-pubescent armpits. *Armpit Coke, ladies?*

"Umm, no thanks," said the one on the right. "We don't drink Coke." I flashed Mom an angry glare. *Way to go, Mom! You fucked up and bought the wrong soda! Now the sister missionaries will never come back!* Looking back on the situation, I might be inclined to think that their refusal of my armpit-warmed Coke would have to do with the bloody stumps that were staining my mother's dishrag. However, it was the following exchange that told me that it was a far more spiritual refusal.

"Yeah," said the one on the left. "You shouldn't be drinking it either. It's loaded with caffeine." I stared at them blankly and shrugged. "It's against our religion."

"Caffeine is against the Word of Wisdom," the one on the right said.

"Yeah," agreed the one on the left. "The prophet said that caffeine is bad for you. That's why we don't drink coffee." My mom nodded in agreement, scooting her cup of coffee next to the ashtray on the floor just out of sight. I attempted to wink at both of them simultaneously, but it just came across as aggressive blinking. I smiled dejectedly and shuffled off back to the kitchen to put the Coke back in the fridge. I cursed myself for not having paid more attention in church as I spent the rest of the night watching professional wrestling in my room and picking glass out of my middle fingers. In a matter of minutes, I had gone from Big Daddy A-Man to Big Daddy A-Hole.

The next day at school found me staring blankly at the chalkboard, mulling over the night before. *Against our religion? Caffeine? Coffee? Why?* The only thing that I could recon is that maybe, at some point, Joseph Smith was having his morning breakfast that one of his child brides cooked for him, and he demanded his cup of coffee be refilled and one of his teetering wives knocked the pot over and burned him in his Articles of Faith. Maybe it was a mistake? The Word of Wisdom is pretty vague on this point. It mentions hot beverages are not good, but herbal tea is ok. What about iced coffee? What if it's decaf? Why would anyone drink it then? And, if hot beverages are indeed outlawed, where does that leave soup? Suppose you have soup in a cup and you drink it at your desk on your lunch break at the insurance company while you contemplate ending all your misery with a well-timed "slip" into traffic? Is soup not a hot beverage if drank from a cup? Would anyone miss you at the insurance company? I have so many questions.

Anyway, our teacher had foolishly brought in a loaf of bread, peanut butter and jelly, and was under the assumption that we would be interested in what he had to say. He started rambling about how fractions could be used to make the 'perfect' peanut butter and jelly sandwich as I found myself drifting back to the sister missionaries. *Against our religion.* That's a pretty big statement. Even at that age, I understood that there was little arguing with that. Religion was heavy. If God said that you couldn't do something, THAT WAS IT! You don't fuck around with the Almighty.

Or do you?

It was at this point my teacher got my attention by waving the heel from the loaf of bread in my face.

"Huh?" I asked, slack-jawed and clearly on another planet.

"I was asking if you minded me using the ends of the loaf to make your sandwich?"

Now, sandwich politics are really not my arena and I really couldn't have cared less about what part of the loaf my sandwich was made on, but I was curious about something. Objects and practices become sacred over vast periods of time. My question was whether or not it was because they were ordained by God or if it was just because people believed it? In short, could people tell when something was *really* holy or if it was being made up? I decided to test how seriously people took religious belief, and like other horrible assholes in history, I decided to use religion to manipulate someone.

"Umm," I said with a shaky voice. "I can't have the ends of the loaf. It's against my religion." The class burst into laughter. The teacher eyed me suspiciously.

"Really?" he scoffed. "And what religion are you, may I ask?"

I turned to him with a sturdy sureness and matched his public-school gaze. *Go for broke,* I thought. "I'm Mormon," I answered. An unexpected hush ran through the class. It was then that I understood that to be Mormon was to be different. That word seemed to carry something with it. Suddenly, I had a very powerful weapon at my disposal.

"Mormon?" he asked softly. I nodded sternly. "Why can't Mormons have the ends of a loaf of bread?" he asked carefully.

"That's where the devil holds it when he helps bake it in the oven," I improvised. The class looked at me like I was crazy, but I held firm. The teacher scoffed. I doubled down. How far could I take this, I wondered? "That's what the Prophet Joseph Smith said." I knew enough to throw 'the prophet' in there a couple of times. It really sells the whole 'against my religion' shtick. "Look, if you want to go against the word of the prophet, that's on you!"

"I'm sorry," he said earnestly. "I had no idea that you were so devout. That's a really wonderful thing to see someone so young involved in church." He put the sandwich that he made for me aside and pushed over the one that he made for himself, sans crusts. Looking back, I can see that he was trying desperately to avoid some kind of lawsuit.

It was on that day I learned two very valuable lessons:

1. *The average person knows next to nothing about the Mormon religion and are too afraid to ask.*

2. *You can get away with a lot of shit if you preface it with,* "My religion says…"

Religion has been used as an excuse for some of the grandest atrocities in the history of the world, there is no denying that. Manifest Destiny, the Crusades, the Spanish Inquisition, and the Mountain Meadows Massacre are but a few examples of "My religion says…". As a child, I was discovering things about religion that would later lead me out of the church and ultimately out of theism. I was slowly starting to understand that there was only power or legitimacy behind something if *you* put it there. God had nothing to do with it. *The Boogey Man only exists if you never turn on the light.*

With Mormonism, I started to understand that our practices and ritual were unique simply because we were the only ones who did it, not because they were ordained by God. Not drinking caffeine has nothing to do with God. It has everything to do with man. If God really gave a shit if you drank caffeine, then he wouldn't have made it. Or, he would have made everyone in the Mormon church allergic to it to show that he really wanted them in his church.

What bothered me the most out of my little experiment was that if I could manipulate someone using religion or God as an excuse, might there be others doing it too? Might those people be in my own church? Might they be the people who founded the church? Later on, when I started researching the many wives of Joseph Smith and Doctrine and Covenants 132, I saw the same kind of manipulation. You say something outlandish, back it up with "It was from God", and you hope everyone buys it. If anyone questions you, buckle down and stand your ground. Make sure you call them faithless, godless, and an apostate. Eventually, they'll either give up or get killed by an extremist.

I played the Mormon card on and off for a few years, usually when I didn't wanna do something. Realistically speaking, it was the beginning of the crumbling of religious thought for me. I just needed help from someone to really kick down those doors. Luckily for me, I was about to be introduced to such a person.

Part Two
I Was a Teenage Mormon!

"And I would just like to leave a word of counsel to the young women of the Church, that a lot of young men in this Church have done very good things with their lives because young women in this Church wanted them to."

- Elder Jeffrey Holland, Church News, July 9, 1994

"Wives, submit yourselves unto your own husbands, as unto the Lord. For the husband is the head of the wife... as the church is subject unto Christ, so let the wives be to their own husbands in every thing."

- "Prophet" Joseph Smith, Jr., 1st President of the Church of Jesus Christ of Latter-day Saints

Chapter 5

Losing My Religion

One of the greatest teachers I ever had was one that I never got a chance to meet. Well, I suppose I met him, but in an offhand way. I'll set the scene. It was fall in Youngstown, Ohio. I was 15. The legendary Stambaugh Auditorium was bursting at the seams and buzzing excitedly. I stood in line next to one of my fellow noisemakers from the band, smoking cigarettes that we bought off a kid in an Indians hat and a camouflage t-shirt. Those stupid details all became important to me because, well, it was an important night. We were there to see George Carlin.

I eagerly pushed my way through the door, past the ticket taker, and went right down to the front. I don't know how we got those seats, but I wanna say thank you to my friend's mom and her amazing ticket purchasing timing. He started the night with a big 'Fuck You!' to everyone and uproarious applause. It was glorious. His set was bleak, nihilistic, and darker than most of the people were prepared for. I gobbled all of it up!

At one point during a joke, he looked me dead in the face and said 'Motherfucker', and I can honestly say that it was the greatest moment of my life at that point. It still might be, come to think of it. I mean, my wedding day was cool and the birth of my son is something I'll always cherish or whatever, but George Carlin gave me a 'Motherfucker'! That's special! St. Carlin had blessed me. It was the culmination of many hours of studying his comedy. I read his books, owned every album, and saw every stand-up special. I even rolled the dice and watched Jersey Girl! To me, his stand-up wasn't just funny; it *meant* something. It made a lot of confusing and scary things in my world start to make sense. It helped on a very deep and personal level.

My introduction to Carlin was something of a clandestine operation. I had snuck down to my older brother's spider-infested room in the basement that he shared with the water heater. There was an old Zenith in there that my Opa had gotten as collateral on a loan that was never repaid. My brother was busy losing at Duck Hunt and was about to throw the controller against the water heater when he remembered that it was time to put on HBO. His eyes lit up as he recalled all the wonderful and perverse programming that came along with it. HBO in the 90s was a reckless wasteland of Real Sex, Taxicab Confessions, Perversions of Science, and of course, the stand-up of George Carlin. My brother and I peeled the spiders off the screen, put the volume down low so that we wouldn't arouse suspicion, and hunkered down for some comedy. Once again, it was a hit. Carlin ranted about stupid people, sex, death, and most importantly, religion.

Oddly enough, it was the religion bits that always made me uncomfortable as a kid. I knew that he was telling jokes, but he always seemed to mean what he said when he talked about religion. I tried to justify it as a kid by telling myself, "Well, that's because he doesn't go to the church I do. If he talked with Brother Mooreman and the bishop, they could help him out." I was a stupid child. However, I was about to be educated.

As I grew up, I kept listening to Carlin. The more I listened, the more I understood what he was saying. I understood that he was using comedy as a means to communicate not only his opinions about the world and the country, but about life as well. I spent less time laughing and more time nodding my head. He was able to explain very complex and scary thoughts in a way that I could not only be comfortable with, but I could understand. Through Carlin, I learned about existentialism, nihilism, and atheism. Most importantly, he made all this stuff funny. It's hard enough for an American to dwell on these subjects. We aren't built for this level of seriousness in life. By wrapping it up in humor, Carlin was able to help others access these thoughts, enriching and enlightening his audience. It's what all great comedians from Lenny Bruce to Richard Pryor have done. All of this came to a head when I entered adolescence.

As I said, I never really had a tight group of friends in church, so Sundays were not my favorite day of the week. In addition, I had started a new school after New Year's break and had no time to make friends. I was alone a lot, and as a result, I spent a lot of time listening to Carlin on cassette because I knew that he knew what it was like to be the weirdo. I think that I adopted many of his views and philosophies as a way to keep myself safe in school and church—two places where I didn't feel safe.

Using the philosophies of Carlin, I began to think of God as an individual, as an institution, and as an idea. If God were an individual, as professed in the Mormon Church, then he clearly does not love each and every one of us as he proclaimed. If he did, why did he create such disparity between individuals in my neighborhood? Why were some people in the church rolling in cash when others were on food stamps? Did God have no sense of justice? The answer was that there is no God and that religion was created to keep society intact and to keep people in line.

God as an institution had no logic either. If all the people on Earth were children of God, why were there so many conflicting reports on what he wanted done? Why, for instance, are there so many different religious texts for one God? Why would he want his day of rest to be on Sunday for Christians, Friday for Muslims, and Saturday for Jews? Was there a miscommunication between his children? If so, isn't it a parent's responsibility to communicate with their children? Why do so many prayers go unanswered? Does God not care? Is he too busy? Is he busy watching MonsterVision with Joe Bob Briggs?

Bringing up God as an idea was also problematic for my young mind. Suppose that God was more of an idea and was not, in fact, "real". That would make the Bible, the Book of Mormon, the Koran, the Torah, and all other scripture meaningless. In which case, how would we define God? How would we decide what was God's commandment or idea and what was man's? Are they the same? What happens if I think of something before God does? Like, if I say that driving on icy roads is bad, then a prophet tells me that God said that driving on the icy road was bad; did I have more insight than God? Did God copy off of me? Am I God? You see how thinking about this stuff fucks with the logic of religion? Now you can start to understand why Mormons hate "intellectuals".

As you can imagine, by asking these questions, I found myself increasingly more isolated in church and school. The school I went to was small, white, and very, VERY Christian. Asking these questions made people uncomfortable. Worst of all, it made them scared. When white people in a small town get scared, that makes life dangerous, so I got into a lot of fights. In a stupid attempt to feel safe, I started bringing a knife with me to school. Luckily, I never had the guts to use it. Where was the love that Christians professed to have? Reality was a depressing nightmare. If that was the Christian life, I wanted no part of it. I tried to isolate as much as I could, simply because being lonely was preferable to being judged. I "acted weird" as a way to let people know not to fuck with me. As a result, I would get called a Satan worshipper and a faggot because I didn't like or respect the feverish religiosity of the world around me. As an adult, I still get judged very harshly when I mention that I am an atheist. There is a lot of anger toward atheists, mainly because a lot of religious folk don't know what the fuck it means.

Because they don't know, they are afraid. Fear leads to violence. I sound like Yoda.

When you are an adolescent and going through this, you tend to do what I do—you lie about stuff. I would say that I believed the church was true during my talks as a way to calm any fears that my family or church leaders had. I would "share my testimony" with the bishop and Brother Mooreman. I would go to the temple when I was older. I would do whatever was necessary in order to keep people from getting to know what was really happening inside of me. I would build a mask of compliance and wear it every Sunday. The questions didn't go away, though. It's something that ex-Mormons call 'Breaking the Shelf'. Basically, the idea is that there is a shelf inside your mind, and when you hear something in church that doesn't make sense or is in conflict with something that you believe, you put that idea on your 'shelf' to deal with it later. Eventually, the shelf gets so overloaded with moral conflicts, textual issues, and logical fallacies that it breaks and your faith is shattered. My shelf wasn't just breaking the Mormon religion, but theism altogether.

I wish I could say that this was an isolated experience and that no other Mormon goes through this. I wish I were the only one. But I am not. This experience is very typical for a lot of former Mormons and former religious people. Some of us come out on the other side benefiting from our experience. We gain an insight into ourselves that we would not have otherwise. We go on to help those transitioning out of faith. We try to educate others on religious and non-religious tolerance. None of us come out unscathed, however.

Adolescence sucks because, well, it's adolescence. Nothing good happens as a teenager. It sucks even worse when you are in a church that demands a constant pursuit of perfection at the cost of your identity and your mind. Adolescents are naturally curious, but in the church, it *wasn't* ok to ask questions. It *wasn't* cool to be different. When you erect walls around teenagers like that, you kill the part of them that loves to chase truth. That is, unless you have a lifeline. For me, I had George Carlin to help me out of that. For Mormons, it is not cool to question the church, but in the words of George Carlin, "You ain't cool, you're fuckin' chilly, and chilly ain't never been cool."

P.S.

If you are one of those people that think back on high school as 'the good ol' days', then I hope you enjoy your sad Sunday dinners at Applebee's.

Chapter 6

The Incredible Exploding Mr. Fluffums!

There are some moments that are so powerful, so potent, so cursed, that they define an entire experience. Like a song that is summed up in a line or two, you forget the verse but remember the chorus. *Hey, Macarena!* Seminary was like that. It was my Macarena, a horrible tedious experience summed up in one cold morning. We'll get to that in a bit.

Anyway, I started seminary like all (American) Mormons do, in freshmen year of high school. For those of you who are godless heathens and don't know what Mormon seminary is, it's basic scripture study. In Freshmen year, we studied the New Testament in the Bible, Sophomore it was to be the Book of Mormon, Junior year was to be the Doctrine and Covenants and the Pearl of Great Price (that's when the apologetics get *real* good!), and the last was to be the Old Testament as a Senior. That's a whole lotta reading to ask of a teenage boy (like me), who had just discovered gas station porno.

You may ask, when exactly did one find the time to fit in this extracurricular activity of holy study and pondering? *After school perhaps? Maybe on the weekend? A free night during the week?* No, no, no, my dear reader. This was not a weekly activity, but a *daily* one. Our seminary classes were held *before* school. In the *morning*. *Before* the ass-crack of dawn. So, in addition to the three-hour service on Sundays and the weekly home teaching I had to go on, I had another five hours of church. So, altogether, about ten hours a week of my teenage life was being devoted to the church. FUN! How on Earth was I going to find time to sniff glue and listen to Black Sabbath in the middle of all that? I tell ya, some people got no respect for the duties of a teenage weirdo!

Every morning at 5 AM, my alarm would rip me out of my dreams about hitting my principal with a Stone-Cold Stunner and finishing him off with a Tombstone pile driver. I understand that mixing the two most iconic finishers in wrestling history is a cardinal sin, but you can't blame a man for his dreams. Since I was a typical teenager and unable to get to bed at a reasonable hour, I'd drag my severely sleep-deprived ass out of bed and make a feeble attempt to calm my wiry hair, only to give up and let it fly. After loading up my book bag and grabbing my Quad (the collected works of Mormon scripture), I'd stumble down the stairs to the garage where the ferry and ferryman awaited me. I wasn't to cross the river Styx that morning, but the river Mahoning. *Dirty old river!*

Of my two parents, my dad was the one who woke up the earliest, so it was his unenviable task to take me to seminary every morning. As I've said, my dad only says three words, so you can imagine the stellar conversations we had at 5 AM.

Alan: Gee, Dad, it's early.

Dad: Yep.

Alan: The sun's not even up.

Dad: Nope.

Alan: Have we ever had a conversation where I wasn't just stating the obvious?

Dad: Shit!

The crumbling Chevy chugged along the road, its headlights blaring into the black morning. I had thought about breaking the awkward silence, but decided against it. Neither one of us wanted to go to church when we didn't *have* to. To Dad, church was for funerals, baptisms, and Christmas (maybe). I can count on one shop teacher's hand how many times I've seen my father in church, which I don't blame him. Only now it was coming back to bite him in the ass. The vacation was over. Mom wrangled him into this adventure. We were together in our misery.

However, we might have been miserable, but at least we didn't have to go hungry. We arrived at a drive-thru that was on the way and my father broke his rule by adding two more words to his lexicon: *black coffee*. He then motioned to me and I ordered breakfast. We ate and drank in silence. Soon, my dad sparked up a cigarette, dragged on it, and flicked the ashes out the window. *Black coffee and cigarettes—the breakfast of champions!*

We arrived at the church and my dad motioned for me to go inside as he clicked on the oldies and lit up another cigarette. I could hear the sounds of Frankie Valli fading away as I stumbled bleary-eyed into the church. The seminary class consisted of myself and about ten other kids. As I was not one who was eager to participate, I found a place somewhere in the back row and hoped that I wouldn't be called on to do anything important. So, naturally, the first thing that happened was that I had to read from the New Testament and discuss how I thought Jesus felt about being crucified. I surmised that Jesus probably did not appreciate the act of being nailed to a chunk of wood, though, as a carpenter, he might have appreciated the irony of being nailed to something that he used to make. The irony was lost on my comrades. It was at this point that I wondered what the Catholic kids were up to at this time in the morning. Probably all snuggled up in their warm beds, dreaming about the Eucharist.

Those mornings were terrible, but for one thing, it afforded me the opportunity to indulge in my adolescent daydreaming. As luck (for me) would have it, only three seats away from me was my secret Mormon crush. You need a crush in church to get you through the day. In fact, I'm fairly certain that in order to be a real teenager, one must have on hand at least three crushes to fit any situation. Anyway, my vision of loveliness was always fixed on her text. She had frizzy curls and a severe overbite. *My kinda girl!* As I drifted in and out of sleep, I envisioned scenes where she and I would face immeasurable odds against all sorts of wonderful creatures. Through our cunning, our brazenness, and our passion for one another, we'd make it out of any scenario I could create. The droning of our seminary teacher would influence the dreams every so often. Once, Ms. Overbite and I were drinking wine at the last supper and we both felt super guilty because Mormons aren't supposed to drink booze. Jesus gave us the ol' thumbs up and we drank till we had our fill.

Since I was frequently engaged on adventures of the mind, it became my father's job to serve as my alarm clock to reality. I'd feel a rough tap on my shoulder, smell the fragrance of non-mentholated cigarettes, and be ripped out of my dreams of adolescent bacchanalia. I'd anxiously check my Dale Earnhardt watch that I acquired from a Wal-Mart parking lot as my dad drove me back home just in time to catch the bus to school. It was a precarious balancing act, one where everything *had* to go according to schedule. If any part of the morning was not in sync, I would be late for school, my father would have to drive me, which would make him late for work, etc. It was a sleepy, anxiety-fueled way to start the mornings of my ninth-grade year.

One morning in mid-November, my father and I were both really tired for some reason. It's almost as if the intensity of early morning church service was starting to catch up with us. Dad had gotten his usual black coffee and I had opted for orange juice instead of chocolate milk that morning. As they say, variety is the spice of life! My bleary eyes looked out across the frigid landscape that is Ohio in November. The dead trees lined the road, shaking their bare limbs in the wind as my dad reached over to get his Zippo from the glove box. Suddenly, from the side of the road shot a white object. It looked like a gigantic dandelion that had gone to seed. I screamed for Dad to stop but it was too late.

"Shit!" he screamed as he slammed on the breaks. It was no use. With a healthy POOF, the object vanished into a flurry of white fur gently floating in the breeze. The car finally skidded to a stop, leaving a skid on the blacktop ten feet long. We both jumped out of the car, our bodies shaking with fear and adrenaline. My mind immediately jumped into the 'what ifs?' *What if it was a kid? Just a little fluffy, furry kid making her way out into the middle of the road at 5:00 in the morning? That might be an overreaction.* I inspected the damage to the front bumper. Aside from a tuft of pink fur and a curious red streak across the hood, there was no damage, not that it would have been noticeable on that shit-box car. I scanned the road for evidence of our victim but could find nothing. However, the look on my dad's face said it all. Toward the rear of the car, I saw what remained of a fluffy white housecat, at least I assume that's what it was. It had pretty much exploded its blood and guts all over the street like a New

Year's Eve confetti cracker. It was like an exploding kitten New Year's Party. *Should old acquaintance be forgot...*

I made my way back to the car, eager to get out of the cold and on with my day. That's when I saw a curious sight that I'd missed on first inspection. It was also the moment that I'd lost my appetite for orange juice forever. Sitting in the middle of the road, facing the car that had just destroyed its mortal carriage, was the severed head of the cat. Dad stomped on the gas, sending us careening away from the scene as fast as possible. His shaky hand lit his unsteady cigarette as he swigged black coffee simultaneously. I searched for something poetic to say to try to calm us both down from the fact that we just atomized a fluffy white house cat. Unfortunately, teenage minds are not known for tact.

"Did you see it's fuckin' head in the middle of the street! Jesus Christ!" I blurted out.

Dad nodded and said, "Yep."

"I thought we'd hit a kid!"

"Nope."

I sighed. "Thank God. I mean, it's sad, but at least it wasn't a human." I paused for a moment as a dreaded realization came over me—cats are usually pets. Pets have owners. *Shiiiiiiit!* "I bet someone will probably look for that little cat. It looked pretty well taken care of."

"Yep," answered Dad with a quaver in his voice.

"Probably a little girl," I speculated. "It looked like a cat a five-year-old might have."

"Yep."

"What do you name a cat like that? Probably something like...I dunno, Mr. Fluffums," I surmised. "That's what I would name him. Little kid will probably wake up; notice her cat is gone, run outside to look for him. Probably call *'Mr. Fluffums! Mr. Fluffums! Where are you?'* Then she'll see that fucking head in the middle of the street! That won't be good..."

"Nope," answered Dad as he lit another cigarette on the end of his current one. The church came into view, as dark and desolate as ever. As I exited the car, I looked back to see my father's face, washed in guilt and horror, illuminated by the warm glow of his cigarette. *Maybe I could get him a card or something,* I thought, *take his mind off of the horror show he created.* I walked inside, still thinking about that cat's head in the middle of the road. It was curious how instantaneous it was. *Poof! That's that. No more chasing mice for you!* Would it be painful to be exploded? Mr. Fluffums didn't exactly have a look of pain on his decapitated head. Actually, it appeared to be more of an expression of confusion. *What the fuck just ripped my head clean off?*

I looked at my Dale Earnhardt watch. Five minutes late. *Whatever.* I pushed my way in and noticed that some preppy-looking asshole with a color-coded Bible had taken my usual seat. I scowled at that bleach-blonde goon and looked for another seat. Wouldn't you know it, only one was available and it just so happened to be right smack next to Ms. Overbite with the frizzy hair. *Perfect!* The one day I might have a chance to talk to her, maybe show her that I'm not a complete asshole, I can't because I got cat-murder PTSD. I placed myself next to her and did my best to make a friendly nod. Either she didn't notice or didn't care, and honestly, I couldn't blame her. I wasn't exactly Marty Mormon and I did smell like cigarettes and black coffee in the morning. Instead of trying to engage in a scripture study, I felt that it might be best for the processing of trauma if I got some shuteye.

I fell back into my normal dream cycle about Ms. Overbite and I on another adventure, only this one was stained with the blood and fur of the massacre I had just been witness to. Her and I were lost in a desert land, searching for one another. A high lonesome voice rang out across the barren landscape.

"Mr. Fluffums! Where's my little cat?" I ran, searching for Ms. Overbite, looking behind cacti and rocks. *If only I had some light*, I thought. The moon rose behind me and illuminated my path. I turned to say thanks to Mother Moon, only to realize that it wasn't the moon, but the floating decapitated head of Mr. Fluffums! Its confused stare and violent hiss shook me to my core. Ms. Overbite was hanging on to the bits of fur where its neck used to be. She was shouting down words of anger and sorrow, for it was *HER CAT!*

"Never again will I give myself to your murderous ways!" she wailed, matching the shrill meows coming out of the giant floating cat head as it chased me through the Joshua Trees and cacti. *Would nobody wake me from this nightmare?*

There was a loud crash. Every eye in the room turned to the door. My dad stood in the doorway, a terrified look on his face and a coffee in his hand. I jolted out of my chair and onto the lap of Ms. Overbite, who summarily pushed me onto the floor. I looked at my watch. Dad looked at his. We looked at each other.

"SHIT!" we shouted. We were late. *Very* late.

I scrambled out the door with my dad pushing me along. Apparently, he had also fallen asleep, probably dreaming of decapitated cats as well. Dad pushed the Chevy's engine to its brink, sending it speeding into the rising sun, running over several small squirrels in the process. We had no time to mourn. We would have plowed through an enchanted forest full of magical singing critters if we had to. I was about to miss the bus. I could see its yellow frame rolling forward away from our driveway. Dad slammed on the breaks, turned the car, pulled a Vin Diesel, and blocked the road, stopping the bus from pulling on without me. I ripped my book bag out of the car, gave my father a thumbs up, and rushed onto the bus. I watched his car peel away as he lit another cigarette and sped away towards his day.

After that day, my dad and I both decided that seminary, while a fine idea, was not exactly for me and that I didn't have to go anymore.

Chapter 7

How I Ruined the Columbus Temple Trip

It is said that one of the most sacred and special things that a Mormon can engage in is *temple work*. It is considered an essential and sacred duty that everyone in the church should participate in *if they are worthy*. It is the place in which you are connected most to the being and presence of God. In fact, it is said that if you are pure of heart and open yourself to it, you can actually see the face of God in the temple. The temple is also where a lot of weird shit happens. Baptisms for the dead, endowment ceremonies, sealings, and 'second anointings' are a few of the strange things that the church keeps out of public knowledge...for the most part. Recently, thanks to the internet, any one of you fine and honorable people can (after reading this book, of course) search for any of the things mentioned and get video proof of the sacred wackiness. For me, my experience at the Mormon Temple in Columbus, Ohio was…well, not so sacred.

It all began a few weeks after I turned 13, a ripe old age to be doing temple work. My seminary teacher had brought it to seminary and had steadily taken the opportunity to work it into her lessons about the New Testament.

"You see, Jesus loved doing temple work! It was an important part of his life! Hopefully, you'll all do the kind of work that Jesus did," she'd say with a satisfied grin.

"Wait, didn't Jesus run up in the temple, flipping over tables and beating people?" I asked with a quizzical look. That's how they handle shit in the hood. *You fuck that temple up, Jesus!* On cue, I'd get the mighty Mormon stare down. *Relax,* I thought, *don't ask questions. Just consume product.*

In any case, all that you could hear in the hallways on Sunday was the excited buzz about the temple trip. For Mormon adolescents, going to the temple means that you will be doing baptisms for the dead. For those who don't know what the hell I am talking about, baptisms for the dead are where an individual—both male and female—gets baptized by proxy for someone who is dead. The idea is that even though these people are dead, they need us living folk to get baptized in their name so that they can get into one of the three heavens that Mormons believe are out there. Sound weird and creepy? Well...it is. So, there. In the past, there has been some controversy over the practice. For instance, there was a time where people were getting baptized in the name of people who had been killed in the Holocaust. You can imagine how well the families of these individuals took it when some white kid in Utah was bringing their murdered family member into the Mormon church without consent. Once it got out, the church vowed to not baptize any more Holocaust victims. No, instead, they baptized Adolf Hitler instead. Think I'm joking? Look it up.

Hitler aside, this baptism for the dead is kind of a rite of passage for young Mormons. It's like when you level up in Mario. You've shown God that you are willing to go to ridiculous lengths in order to please your family! Many proud parents stood around the halls, beaming about their child's first temple trip. I passed by, getting a few scowls and scoffs, but mostly, I got the question: *ARE YOU GOING TO THE TEMPLE*?

I froze on the spot, the entire congregation staring at me. Everyone, from the old white Bishop to the young white babies, bore holes into my head with their obsessive glares. I backed up into the wall as the hungry crowd surrounded me. It reminded me of the torch and pitchfork scenes from the old monster movies and I felt just like Boris Karloff. *Fire bad, temple good!*

Once again, the question was posed: *ARE YOU GOING TO THE TEMPLE?*

"I…I don't know," I said meekly. "I guess…I have to ask my mom." The crowd was ravenous! They could smell the indecision in the air and they sank their teeth into me.

I heard a voice cry out, "His mom! Let the boy ask his mom!" They shuffled me through the hall, pushing me along those corrugated walls till we reached the doors of the ward library.

My mom looked at the hungry crowd. I tried to shrink myself with no success because I was being hoisted up by two taller boys.

"Crap, what did he do now?" she sighed. I felt a nudge in my back by one of the taller boys, who glared with threatening encouragement. I turned to face my mom.

"Hey, Mom, um...you know there is a temple trip coming up...you mind if I go along?" I squeaked out. The eyes of the collective descended on my mom. However, my mom didn't play that shit. Instead, she stood her ground and glared right back at them.

"Is one of you gonna drive him?" she shot back at the stunned crowd. The bishop stepped forward.

"Of course, Sister. We are going to carpool together. We are probably going to stop at Burger Time Burgers afterwards and get vanilla milkshakes." He smiled pleasantly, probably thinking about those milkshakes.

My mom looked back at me and nodded. "It's fine with me. Have fun." The crowd gave me a great '*Hurrah!*' and clapped me on the back and went back to their own devices.

I stood in the thinning crowd, feeling a hot wave of embarrassment and wondering just what I had gotten myself into. In school, I had heard about peer pressure potentially luring me into the world of drugs, but I had no idea that the same could be said about religion. Same tactics with one vital difference—drugs *actually* give you something for your money.

My Bishop, milkshakes still on his mind, asked me to accompany him to his office for my *worthiness interview*. You see, in order to go to the temple to do all this awesome work, one must first have a worthiness interview with the bishop in order to get what's called a temple recommend. If you pass, you get a little card that lets you into the temple to do whatever work you are set to do. The thing that really sucks is that you have no idea what to expect when you sign up to do this work, but everyone makes it out to be such a huge deal. So, when you actually get there and see what you're in for…well…it's too late to back out now!

Anyway, back to the interview. This highly awkward and uncomfortable interview occurs with you and this MALE behind closed doors, away from your parents, with no witnesses. Sounds creepy, right? It is. Now, if you were a normal teenager like I was, chances are that you had also been engaged in unsavory activities that were not approved of by the church. Teenage boys have...well...extremely poor control over their...well...let's say that there was a reason I had a Britney Spears poster in my room. I'll give you a hint—*it wasn't because I liked her music!* With this in mind, I had to amend my answers to the bishop as not to arouse suspicion to my suspicious arousals. It was a masterful performance on my part, if I do say so myself. I gotta tell you, and maybe this is something you already know, but it's *fun* to lie to clergy! I mean, sure, it's probably wrong, but if you're like me, lie your ass off! Why not? *The church has been lying a lot longer than you have!*

> **Bishop:** Do you keep the Word of Wisdom?
>
> **Me** (*trying to hide my coffee breath*): You bet!
>
> **Bishop:** Do you live the law of chastity?

Me (*visibly shaking and trying not to burst into flames*): Sure do!

Bishop (*uncomfortably squirming*): Are you sure? That includes masturbation. Do you know what that is?

Hmm, let's see…Spankin' the Tankin? Shaking hands with Beef? Holding close to the Rod?

Me: Yeah, sure. I never touch the stuff!

This seemed to satisfy the bishop enough to where he signed off my temple recommend and set in motion one of the most awkward, embarrassing moments of my adolescent life. The only saving grace is that I can reflect on that day as a truly awkward experience not just for myself, but every single person in attendance at the temple. At least I have that comfort.

The week leading up to the temple trip, our seminary teacher prepped us on temple etiquette for the baptism of the dead. We go in, we get in our snazzy baptism jumpsuit, we go into the water one by one, they read the name of some poor dead schmuck, we get dunked a bunch of times, we get out. Lots of fun. As for the baptism jumpsuit, well, it kinda looks like the later Elvis jumpsuits, except without the gold bell-bottoms and all the rad sequins. It's uncomfortable, awkward, and white. *Super-duper white.* Now, anyone familiar with the motorcycle rally in Sturgis, South Dakota knows that when you toss water on white t-shirts, they tend to become see-through. This is important to note because I sure didn't.

The morning of the trip, the ten of us piled into Brother Mooreman's white Econoline van that he had gladly lent the bishop. I think he was more excited about pimping out his Mormon mass transit than we were to ride in it. Anyway, I pushed myself into the back of the van with three other boys. The girls sat in the row ahead of us. A familiar head of bushy hair parked herself directly ahead of me. It was Ms. Overbite, the object of my affection. I gave her a polite nod and smile, which she returned. *Hmm, not exactly a proclamation of love, but better than a nut punch!* She had warmed significantly to me since she found out I was headed to the temple. Well, progress is progress. *Let's see if I can maintain this brief window of goodwill.* Off we went three hours southwest to Columbus, city of

114

dreams! Three hours is a long time for a 13-year-old and there is only so much 'I Spy' one can play with their contemporaries, so I popped Kiss into my CD player, and my mind went over the temple lore that I had heard.

For instance, I was told that some people have claimed to have seen the face of God in the temple. That's heavy shit! I wondered if I would be one of the lucky ones to see the face of God. If so, that might change my burgeoning Atheism. I wondered if seeing the face of God was maybe like one of those illusion pictures, the kind where you stare at it long enough and you see a sailboat. Or maybe God would be a giant floating head. I kept thinking of where I might see the face of God. Maybe in the foyer? Maybe in the hallway? Maybe in the marble of the walls? Or, maybe God would pop out of the front door like Jacob Marley. *Why do you doubt your senses?!* For the first time, I was actually excited about church. I made sure to keep my mind open.

We arrived at the temple and made our way through the vast doors, which, unfortunately, did not bear the face of God. I was overwhelmed by the amount of marble, gold, and light the place had. It looked like a mansion in heaven. It was incredibly quiet and all the temple workers were wearing these funky white outfits. It smelled different too, like a hotel pool. I would find out why in a bit. It was a strange experience just walking through the door, so you can imagine my surprise when the temple workers came over and started to separate us. The boys were ushered to one side, the girls to another, and we were given the *temple spiel.*

"This is a sacred duty Heavenly Father has called you here to do. You are going to be baptized in the name of those who are dead. They are waiting for you to do this so that they might enter the kingdom of Heaven!" said the temple worker in an ethereal whisper. Ok, this sounded like cool shit! I was pumped! I could ignore the slightly eerie atmosphere if it meant helping someone out. Let's help these poor floating spirits get into heaven!

We went into the blindingly white changing rooms where we put on our non-Elvis approved baptism jumpsuits and waited for our cue to go out into the baptism area. The smell of hotel pool was getting stronger. I surmised that it must have something to do with the baptisms. Our Bishop was in the changing room with us, keeping the silence and reverence amongst us boys. *Maybe I would see the face of God underwater. It's a thought.* Another thought that I had was how odd it was that all the boys seemed to have something in common, something that I did not— everyone was wearing white underwear. *That's gross,* I thought. *Why would anyone wear tidy whities anymore? That's a little creepy.* I finished zipping up the jumpsuit over my black boxers and stood by the door.

"Woah, you can't wear that!" called one of the boys. "Dude, weren't you listening in seminary?"

"What's your problem?" I asked. I had the same ridiculous jumpsuit on that he did. I was just trying to see God, just like every other asshole in this place.

"He's right," agreed another boy. "You <u>have</u> to wear white in the temple."

"What are you talking about?" I said. That's when I understood.

Oh, fuck, I was supposed to wear white underwear! It all came back to me. The week leading up to the temple visit, the week where my seminary teacher was harping on us to prepare, she also mentioned that we had to wear white underwear. I had tuned her out so well that I hadn't remembered till that very moment. I looked down and could see my boxers clear as day through my jumpsuit. Hot embarrassment leaped over me, producing instant swamp-ass. I was stuck.

"Wh-what should I do?" I asked as I was sweating bullets.

"Dude, you are gonna have to go commando," they said in unison. Thinking back on it, it's a little disconcerting that they were so involved in my underwear situation, but I had no time. I was terrified. How bad would it be to piss off God by wearing black boxers in his house? Would lightning strike me? Maybe he would give me a heart attack? Worst of all, suppose nothing happened. Suppose that I get baptized for all those people, but it's nullified because I was wearing the wrong kind of underwear.

Picture all those floating dead spirits, hanging out at the door of heaven, not able to get in because I had the wrong underwear on. *Not cool.* I pulled off my jumpsuit, flung off my black boxers, zipped myself back up, and got in line as we were being shuffled out into the baptism area. *Deep breath,* I thought. *It's not like it could get any worse.*

The smell of hotel pool was front and center as I took in the scene of the baptismal font. I took in the full picture of the temple and I immediately felt very uncomfortable. The whiteness of everything, from the marble to the clothes made me feel like I was in a mausoleum. The only bit of color came from the large statues of 12 golden oxen that held up the baptismal font on their backs. I observed the heavenly agony on each of their faces, straining against the weight of the font, but knowing it was for a good cause. I immediately thought of Charlton Heston in the Ten Commandments throwing down the tablets at the feet of those worshiping a golden calf. *Don't think,* I thought, *just go with it.* The girls were already waiting, sitting reverently with their hands on their knees, a serene smile on most of their faces. Ms. Overbite looked particularly lovely with her frizzy hair tied back into a tight ponytail. *Don't think about her,* I told myself. *These jumpsuits don't leave much to the imagination and you are already playing with a handicap. The last thing you want is visible proof that you lied in your Worthiness Interview.* We boys took our seats and I did my best to manage my wobbly bits.

The MAN performing the baptisms entered, gave his spiel, and we began. The first to go in was one of the boys who "saved" me from embarrassing myself in my black boxers. He went into the Baptismal Font, all adorned with oxen, and the process began.

"Brother Bruder, for and in behalf of Saul Rosenberg, who is dead, I baptize you in the name of the Father, and of the Son, and of the Holy Ghost. Amen." Brother Bruder went into the water with a healthy splash. "Brother Bruder, for and in behalf of Esther Rosenberg, who is dead, I baptize you in the name of the Father, and of the Son, and of the Holy Ghost. Amen." Another healthy splash, this time, barely enough time to breathe. *This is a little excessive,*

I thought. *If you drown the guy, that means extra work for the rest of us.*

On and on he went, dunking this poor guy till he had baptized a whole family of formerly Jewish people. The poor guy marched back to the changing room sopping wet, wiping baptism water out of his face. Two more young men went forth, both getting dunked for the dead, when suddenly…

"Brother Young, it's your turn," said the bishop. I could see that he felt calm and relaxed. Maybe he was looking at the face of God right now. Maybe he was thinking about those milkshakes he promised. I marched past the boys, past the girls, past Ms. Overbite, and right to the font. I took a deep breath, sucking in that holy pool water smell, and was ready. I stepped down into the pleasantly warm water, assumed the position, and prepared for the dunking. *Let's do this,* I thought. *Let's get this over with so that I can get some milkshakes.*

"Brother Young, for and in behalf of Fritz Merkel who is dead, I baptize you in the name of the Father, and of the Son, and of the Holy

Ghost. Amen." Under I went. The water matted my mop of curly hair to my face. A couple of short breaths and I went under again. *Shit,* I thought, *I hope these people I'm getting baptized for appreciate this. I'm about to pass out. Focus,* I told myself. *Milkshakes are a-comin'. Let's see if this scores me any points with Ms. Overbite.* I could just make out her wavy form through the glaze of the baptism water. *Boy, she really does look lovely.* My thoughts focused on her as I went under the water again and again, each time for a different German who I would later find out were all related to me. I must have baptized half the dead people of Nuremberg. Each time I went under, I thought of Ms. Overbite, running into my arms in a meadow somewhere. We'd embrace passionately, enjoying each other's presence. *Boy, this water is really nice.*

"Thank you so much, Brother Young. You did good work today." I snapped back to reality. There I was, face to face with the man in white who was nodding toward the steps to get out of the baptismal font. He had lots of dead people to get through today and he clearly did not have time for me to fuck around in his hot tub anymore. *Cool! I'll just pop out of the water like a...oh no!* I looked down in horror at the reality I was facing. The wet white fabric had turned translucent and was clinging to my chest. Instantly, my body became aware of the shift from warm water to cold air and it reacted in kind. I will let you, dear reader, figure out what that means. The more steps that I took out of the warm water and into the cold world, the more my body reacted to it. *Jesus, I feel naked,* I thought.

On her way to the baptismal font was my beloved Ms. Overbite, her frizzy hair bouncing playfully as she made her way. I finished climbing the stairs out of the water, watching her dreamily as she approached the edge. Our eyes locked. I smiled, hoping to relay my appreciation for her loveliness, her serene perfection. She looked into my eyes, taking in my wet and shaking form. Her serenity turned to horror. She stepped back from the baptismal font. She obviously did not feel the same way. My heart sank. *I get it,* I thought, *but this is a bit harsh. Why the horror?* I became aware of my body, the sinking feeling I felt, the absolute cold of the fabric against my skin. Then, I noticed that she was not the only one who had that expression on her face. Everyone seemed to be staring at me horror-stricken. Why? Must my love life be horrific not only to myself, but to others?

Remember what I said earlier about what happens when you toss water on white fabric? Remember what I said earlier about me going commando? It turns out that everyone else in the temple was slowly becoming savvy to that fact. There I stood in the middle of the temple, soaking head to toe in a white jumpsuit that was now transparent. My glorious big white ass-cheeks shone through the fabric in ultra-HD. My dear Ms. Overbite, unfortunately, was whacked full in the face with my full Monty. That poor girl. Her first time seeing a penis and it had to be mine. They don't make apology cards for that kinda stuff. I instantly threw my hands over my…you know, and rushed off to the changing room. My heart was slamming against my chest. A cold sweat had broken out. I was utterly mortified, absolutely embarrassed. My quaking hands removed the jumpsuit and tossed it on the floor. I pulled my clothes on without even drying off. I thought about hiding in one of the lockers or maybe running away to start a new life in Cambodia. Anything, just so that I didn't have to face a three-hour van trip with a bunch of people who just got to see man-land.

One by one, the other boys came in, sopping wet, each of them looking at me like I owed them money. In an effort to avoid the indignity of them having to look at me, I fixed my gaze to the ceiling, to the windows, to the tiles on the floor, anywhere they weren't looking. It was there, in the corner of the temple changing room, where I found the face of God. He was giving me the middle finger.

I was the first to make my way back to the white Econoline van. I sat in the back, disheartened and emotionally wrecked. I shoved my headphones on and hit the play button, only to find out that my batteries had died. Yet another nut punch from the Lord. The bishop latched himself into the driver's seat. He looked through the rear-view mirror at me. I got the distinct impression that he felt like I had let him down. Maybe I did. Had I let down the dead people that I got baptized for too? Would they haunt my dreams, shouting German obscenities at me? *Well, if that was the case, I might be able to finally learn German,* I thought. *Need to learn a language fast? Disgrace your ancestors and get taught from the finest ghouls and goblins this side of the veil! Make the best out of a bad situation!*

"That was…not…" he started. He struggled to find the correct reassurances that go along with a boy of 13 showcasing his ass-cheeks and bobblehead in the holiest of holies. "You know, I think we'll get milkshakes another day."

Chapter 8

Chewing Crack Rocks in The Baptismal Font

It's not uncommon for teenagers, especially during the late 90s and early 00s, to define themselves by very rigid characteristics. Some find themselves defined by their clothes or what church they go to, others by the sports they play, and some define themselves by their academic powers. I defined myself by music. It made life simple and safe enough that I could navigate around the major conflicts (internal and external) that might arise. That's how it was for a while. I muddled through church alone, keeping to myself, but always having some kind of music playing in my brain. Sometimes it would be my own, but most of the time it was the music of the masters. Miles Davis co-mingled with Megadeth while Public Enemy played chess with

Rush. On occasion, a tune that I was hoping to write made its way into the front, begging for the half-completed lyrics to be finished when we got home. I could feel the song wanting to come out and be plucked to life on the strings of my beloved. Whenever I felt alone, I reached into my brain and pulled out the appropriate music. I still do. However, there are times when you find yourself in a position where someone else wants to jam.

It was a typical dreary Sunday in Warren, Ohio, land of foreclosed houses and liquid cheese. Sacrament meeting had just let out and the hallway was filled with a multitude of merry Mormons shuffling toward their classrooms for Sunday school. My eyes were cast down at the floor, focusing on the flecks of mud that dotted my Wal-Mart loafers. I was trying to avoid eye contact with my ward for many reasons, one of them being that I had just exposed myself in an alarming fashion at the Columbus temple earlier that month. I didn't even bother to let anyone know that I had turned 14 the Sunday before. Best to keep a low profile, get through the day, and go on with the week. My mind was preoccupied with replaying the baptism debacle when I collided with something bony and rickety.

Two crusty bootleg Adidas sneakers turned toward me as I looked upward to their owner. Standing in front of me was a very skinny, very angry-looking young man with shoulder-length red hair. His eyes cut through me like saw blades and his thin lips curled around a mouth of crooked teeth. Despite his funk-nasty teeth, he was very handsome. *If he never smiles,* I thought, *he could get any girl he wanted.*

"S-sorry," I mumbled to him. His fiery glare fixed on me.

"What?" he shot back. "What for?"

"I…well, I bumped into you just now."

"No, you didn't," he replied.

"Yeah, I th-think I did," I stuttered. He grinned. Was he fucking with me?

"No, you didn't," he said commandingly. "You didn't *bump* into me. Your fat ass *almost knocked me out!* I almost landed in a coma because of you. You should lose some weight so you don't kill anyone else!"

The hot fires of embarrassment washed over me. I was overweight at the time and rather sensitive about the fact. It *really* bothered me. I'd be lying if I said that it didn't. However, there was something else about what he said that bothered me even more.

"I *didn't* kill you," I said.

"What?"

"You said, 'I should lose some weight so I don't kill anyone else,' but I *didn't* kill you. You're still alive...as far as I know." His grin faded.

"Also," I added, "if you were in a coma, you wouldn't be dead. You'd just...you know...be in a coma." He may have been pretty, but he was stupid. *He'll go far in life.*

His wiry frame stepped closer to mine. He pushed his face through my personal space bubble and into the weird-and-creepy realm of closeness. I could smell his breath...I could smell...COFFEE!

"Listen," he said with his reeking coffee breath, "I will kill you, your mom, your dad, your whole mission-loving family if you mess with me. Got it?" He posed for a second, waiting presumably for me to shit my pants and run to the bishop. However, his acrid coffee breath was begging to be made fun of.

"Dude, is that coffee on your breath?" I blurted out. The buzz in the hallway stopped. All eyes turned to the wiry redhead standing in my personal bubble. He turned toward the disappointed gaze of a hundred merry Mormons. With a swish, he was off, leaving me standing against the wall with the lingering smell of coffee breath in my nostrils.

That was fucking weird, I thought as I headed to my class. I had never seen that kid before in my life. He was close to me in age, perhaps a bit older, but I had never seen him at any church functions before. Was he new? Was he visiting? Perhaps not. Perhaps he was Catholic. *That must be it,* I thought. *I'd probably be angry too if I were Catholic and I was in a church with nary a crucifix to be found. Is that why the Elders in the church didn't want us to mix with them?* I hadn't expected to do this much thinking on a Sunday.

I went through my class in an anxious haze. Those angry, pissed eyes kept flashing in my brain. The smell of his coffee breath hit me every time I took a breath. Fear, anger, and tension played kickball with my stomach, and before I had the opportunity to gather my thoughts, class was over. It was time to go back into the shuffle, back to the sea of people that might hold him. Being a teenage boy sucks. I mean, it sucks being a teenager in general, but let me explain why this particular instance sucks for a boy. I was terrified that this kid was going to start some shit with me in the hallway. That's right, *in a church hallway*, where presumably one might feel safe. Now, if I back down and try to keep the peace, I open the door for him to fuck with me for the rest of time. If I beat the shit out of him, I open the door for him to retaliate. If I tell someone, they will blow it off as "Boys being boys", and tell me to "Man up!" If I *don't* tell someone, I get to live in anxiety. There is no winning solution. I suspect that is why so many boys turn to violence. I mean, if the world doesn't care about you, why should you care about it?

The crowd in the hallways started to thin, allowing me to focus more on threat assessment. My eyes engaged in a paranoid scan of the hallway, searching only the way that terrified eyes could. Every step I took, I swore that I could hear something following me—a swishing rattling sound. *What the hell is that? Don't turn around,* I thought. *Don't give him a reason to start shit. It's all in your head.*

Step, step, swish, swish. Step, step, swish, swish. I could hear it. I was certain. The last of the crowd was filing into their classrooms. I could feel the warmth of anonymity giving way to the cold reality of focus. He was there. I could hear him.

"I figured this was safer," he said. *Swish, swish.*

"What?" I replied, still not facing him.

Swish, swish. "Walking behind you." *Swish, swish.*

What the hell was that sound? Curiosity got the best of me. I turned to face him. His crusty bootleg Adidas shoes anchored his wiry frame smack dab in the middle of the hallway. His crooked smile worked its way out from underneath his red hair. In his hand was a weathered and beaten old hacky sack, which absentmindedly tossed and caught. *Swish, swish.*

"I think we got off on the wrong foot," I said, sticking my shaking hands behind my back. "I don't know what happened, but I'd like to be friends."

"Yeah?" he said. "That's nice. Friends are nice." *Swish, swish.*

"Yeah, they are."

"You know what's cool about friends?" he asked with a twitch in his smile as he snatched his hacky sack out of the air.

"No?" *Was he fucking with me again?*

"Friends don't rat on you when you have coffee breath," he whispered.

"What?" I asked. "What are you talking about?"

"I got called into the bishop's office because of that. He lectured me for 20 minutes about the evils of caffeine addiction and how I can never go to the temple with a heart full of hate and a stomach full of coffee."

"That's a bit dramatic, even for the bishop," I muttered.

"Yep." *Swish, swish.*

"Look, I drink coffee too. It's not that big a deal. Everything's good," I said reassuringly. "As for the temple, I don't care for it either. For reasons you can't possibly fathom…"

He nodded and waved the hacky sack at me. "Yeah, well, I guess friends also give friends second chances. So, that's what I'm going to give you. A big ol' fat second chance."

"That's…good?" I said with an uncertain smile.

He nodded and held out his hand in such a way that he looked like a thin, pale, redheaded version of a mafia boss. I approached with trepidation. *Second chance? For what? Do I want to be friends with this guy? He scares the shit out of me,* I thought. *Then again, he seems wary of what's going on around here, so we got that in common. Plus, he might scare the hell out of the others. What the hell! At least I won't have to wonder anymore.*

"Here, this is for you," he said as he shook his balled fist. I put my hand out and he dropped a tiny misshapen lump into my hand. I looked down at it, wondering what the hell it was and what the hell was going on.

"Um, you want me to throw this away for you?" I asked curiously.

"No, you dickhead!" he said in a hushed tone. "Don't you know what that is? Throwing that away is like throwing away gold!"

I looked down at the mishappen gray lump and rolled it around in my hand. "You don't say?"

He sighed. "Obviously you aren't cool enough to know what that is, so I guess I have to tell you." He searched the hallway for wandering ears and leaned in close. I mimicked him, hopeful to show solidarity in our nefarious natures.

"That," he said, "is a crack rock."

My heart sank. Dread filled me. I felt sick to my stomach and instantly broke out in guilt sweats. *A FUCKING CRACK ROCK?! IN CHURCH?!* I saw the judge sentencing us to lengthy terms. I saw myself navigating the vast complex prison system, having to shank a guy in the laundry room for a pack of cigarettes, then having to tunnel out with nothing but a toothpick and the tab from a soda can. *That's a bit far*, I told myself. *Hmm, how do we play this one off? How might we get out of this situation with our dignity intact and only a minor blemish on our legal record?*

"You ok?" he asked with uncharacteristic concern.

"Fine!" I said as I wiped the beads of sweat from my upper lip. "It's all good. Just, you know, thinking 'bout how much I love crack!"

"Ok," he said as he snapped back into character. "Good. See, I'm a big-time drug lord and I don't need no snitches telling on me. Got that?"

"Word," I nodded.

"Good. So, here's what you gotta do if you want to be cool with me. You listening?"

"Word," I nodded again.

He leaned in. "You gotta…you know…DO THAT CRACK!"

"Like, smoke it?" I asked. "I don't have a crack pipe." It was true, I was sans crack pipe. "Could I borrow one?"

"DUMBASS!" he cringed. "You don't smoke crack! I mean, you could, but that's not how this crack is supposed to go."

Really? I thought. *Cause every time I acted up in school, I'm pretty sure my teacher asked if I was* smoking *crack, not* chewing *it. Ehh, what do teachers know?*

"Ok then," I replied. "How is *this* crack supposed to go?"

He turned shiftily towards the bathroom, grinning malevolently. "You gotta go in there and chew it up and swallow it. It's gonna taste terrible. You'll probably go insane, but if you do this, we'll be cool." I was starting to wonder if a person who would willingly give away crack for free was the type of person I would benefit from being cool with.

"Ok," I sighed. "I will go into the bathroom and…chew up this crack rock."

A wide grin broke out over his face. He kicked open the door to the bathroom and flipped on the lights. As I made my way in, he swished his hacky sack, chuckled, and said, "Have a nice trip! Oh, and by the way, if you don't do it, I'll be able to tell. That's some high-quality shit!"

The door shut behind me with a proper 'thunk' and I immediately went to work checking all the stalls for occupants, hoping for any excuse to rush out of the bathroom and away from this crazy crack-rock catastrophe I had gotten myself into. My paranoid mind raced with possible outcomes to this activity. What if there is a massive run on the bathroom and every single male that held the priesthood found me in the bathroom gnawing on a crack rock like a degenerate? *Quick, snuff him out! The boy smells of coffee and crack! We must set him on fire in the dumpster to sanctify our church! Sisters, gather the wood!* What might Mom say about that? Would she help get the wood?

To my right was a door that led to the baptismal font. Every Mormon church has a special baptismal font where the members get baptized by immersion. Think of it like a bathtub that goes about waist-high. Each bathroom has a door that leads to it so that you can get dressed in your bootleg Elvis jumpsuit and get dunked. *That would be a really great place to chew my crack rock,* I thought. I could shut the door and nobody would know I was in there. It was usually locked, but at some point, the door had become warped and the latch no longer lined up properly, so I nudged the door and it swung open with a graceful calm. It was apparent that Heavenly Father wanted me to chew my crack rock in peace.

I descended into the Baptismal Font and pushed the door shut. It was dark, except for a small sliver of light that peeped through the bottom of the door, illuminating the misshapen lump in my hand. *So, this is what I had been reduced to? Preparing myself to crunch down on a crack rock in a baptismal font? Well,* I sighed, *best to get it over with and move on.* I popped the grey misshapen lump into my mouth and chomped down on it with my molars. A horrific jabbing pain accompanied a loud cracking sound.

"Fuck!" I exclaimed. "This hurts my teeth!" *That must be why it's called a crack rock.* I chomped a bit more, hoping that extra saliva might soften the illicit substance. No dice. It remained as hard as Youngstown steel. I spat out the lump into the palm of my hand. It was starting to resemble a dog's chew toy with saliva and teeth marks dotting it. *People do this for fun? Why not just eat a burger and take a nap?* I crawled out of the baptismal font and back into the bathroom. I stared disheartened at the lump in my hand. *This isn't worth it*, I thought. I went over to the toilet, tossed the lump into the water, and kicked the flusher. Maybe the alligators that lived in the sewer might have a better time getting high on crack than I did.

Since I did not ingest the crack rock, I was not high. This was a problem since I knew that the redheaded crack-slinger outside the door would know if I was still sober. It was, after all, "high-quality shit". So, in a move acted out of self-preservation, I had to figure out a convincing crack walk to pass muster. Luckily, I grew up in Warren, so I knew what real crack heads looked and walked like. Usually, they would be between the houses or in the empty lot across from the school, crouched behind a pile of tires, smoking the crack rather than chewing it. I had been able to mimic their walk pretty well as a gag in the fourth grade, so I pulled it out of my bag of tricks. I clenched my teeth like a caveman, kicked one foot sideways, acted like one leg was longer than the other, and popped my eyes open as wide as they could go. I looked in the mirror to see if it looked ok. I looked less like a crack head and more like I had to sneeze.

"Well, it's passable," I said as I went to the door. Sure enough, waiting outside was the redhead, his hacky sack bouncing off of his bootleg Adidas. *Ok, showtime!* I stepped my crooked foot out into the hallway when, suddenly, it erupted with the sound of opening doors, mingled conversations, and shuffling feet. The redhead bounced his hacky sack between his feet, but he faltered and launched his hacky sack into the filling crowd. He lunged for it, but it was too late. It wound up under the bamboo cane of a woman in her 80s. The cane ripped into the cheap fabric of the hacky sack, spilling out hundreds of tiny misshapen grey lumps. *Not lumps, CRACK ROCKS! His stash is in his hacky sack? What balls!*

"DUDE, HOW MANY CRACK ROCKS DO YOU HAVE?!" I exclaimed in shock. The redhead's face turned white with dread. The crowd stopped in their place, their eyes once again trained on the two of us. A figure pushed his way forward, shifting the old lady aside, and towering over the two of us. Our Bishop loomed over us. He looked at the redhead, looked at me, and looked down at the hundreds of crack rocks scattered across the floor.

He shook his head in disappointment. "Both of you, come to my office. Now!"

****

We sat side by side across from the bishop, both of us doing our best to keep our eyes firmly fixed on the floor. Scattered across the desk were about 20 or so of the crack rocks that spilled out of the hacky sack. In all of this, I felt a strange sense of relief that I didn't have to resort to my fourth-grade crack head walk after all.

The bishop eyed us both. "John," he said to the redhead, "were you selling crack rocks again?" *Again? Who* was *this kid?*

John shifted uncomfortably. "No, sir." The bishop eyeballed me.

"It's true," I said. "He didn't sell me the crack rock. I found it." John looked up, surprised. "I'll take the consequences."

The bishop stood up behind his desk and picked up one of the crack rocks. "John, we've talked about you lying to people. Heavenly Father looks down on liars. Here you are, trying to pass off hacky sack beads as crack!"

"Excuse me?" I blurted out. "What was that?"

"That crack rock you took from him was actually a hacky sack bead," said the bishop. "It's a bit of plastic that he'd been kicking around in that nasty ball for Lord knows how long."

I turned slowly to John. His face was the same shade of red as his hair, which led to a bizarre effect. He sort of looked like a fire hydrant. "You gave me a plastic hacky sack bead to chew on? You...fucking...BUTT!" I crossed my arms in disgust. John chuckled slightly.

"LANGUAGE!" cried the bishop. "Well, it's at least reassuring that neither of you know what crack looks like. Thank the Lord for that," he shrugged. "Ok, both of you go home. This is clearly too stupid to get your parents involved. No more crack rocks, you hear?"

He pushed us both out into the hallway, alone to finish any conflicts on our own terms. John, that redheaded goon, had lied to me and given me a crusty piece of plastic to chew on to get high. It was one of many high-water marks in the stupidity of my teenage years. I turned to John and grimaced. He gave me a sheepish smile from under his red hair.

"Look," he started, "I was just messing with you. I thought you were, you know," he gestured toward the bishop's office, "one of them."

"Well, I'm not," I said. "There are better ways to find out than offering someone fake crack rocks."

He nodded. "I guess. Well, I gotta go. I'll see you next week."

"Yeah," I nodded. "Later."

John stopped and turned. "You think someone else would fall for it?"

I thought for a second. "Hmm, maybe one of the Mooremans. If we don't get one, we can just move on down the line." At that moment, we both got the same mischievous smile across our faces. And that, folks, is how I met my best friend, Crack Rock Johnny.

Chapter 9

The Mighty Mormon Jam Session!

Crack Rock Johnny and I were pretty tight from the ages of 14-16, bonding mostly over our mutual desire to be literally anywhere else on a Sunday than at church. The irony is that we both looked forward to Sundays now. We had begun our reign of terror against the mormiest of the Mormon kids in our class and continued outside at various social functions. We'd run through the halls screaming about a fire in the dumpster or raving about an alligator running loose in the nursery. One time, we glued loose change on the floor of the hallway and laughed hysterically as people tried to pick it up. During the ward basketball competition, I put Johnny on my shoulders and we pretended to be a really tall guy, and terrorized all the legit basketball players.

It got so bad that I think everyone in the ward just gave up trying to stop us. Let that be a lesson, kids: people will give up on you if you piss them off enough. Anyway, on Sundays, we'd meet up in the hallway after services and head to Sunday school, sit in the corner, and trade CDs. If you know what CDs are, welcome to old age!

One Sunday, Johnny brought me out to his family's beat-up station wagon and showed me a giant tan guitar case that was covered in skater stickers and a Marilyn Manson sticker featuring him in his *Mechanical Animals* prosthetics. I ogled the case because I knew what was inside.

"That's gotta be a bass guitar!" I said, eagerly rubbing my hands together.

Johnny flipped his hair out of his face and shrugged. "What makes you think it's a bass? It *could* be a 1969 Stratocaster instead."

"Johnny, you can't even *spell* Stratocaster," I quipped.

"Neither can you!" he shot.

"You're a bastard and that's a bass guitar," I said, trying to paw my way into the case.

"You wanna bet money on it?"

"I would if I had any," I retorted. He snickered and flipped open the case. Sure enough, inside was a very cheap, very red bass guitar. The tuning pegs were loose, the strings were covered in a brown crust, and the bridge was hanging on by two stripped screws.

"See, I told you. Stratocaster!" said Johnny pointing at the shitty bass. "I bet you feel pretty stupid right now."

"No, I'd feel stupid playing that thing!" I said with a look of disgust. "Jesus, dude, just looking at this thing is gonna give me a disease!"

"Well, I got one from your mom last night, so we'll call it even."

"Touché," I nodded. "Johnny, I play bass. I know what a bass looks like. That red, shaky, herpes encrusted piece of shit is ABSOLUTELY NOT a Stratocaster." Johnny's face fell as I picked up the bass and started making adjustments.

"Ah, whatever," said Johnny. "It's been hanging out in the attic since I was a kid. A family of bats were making a home in the case. We were going to drop it off at Larry's Super Pawn later. I'm hoping to trade it in for a new snare drum."

"You're a drummer?" I asked. He nodded. "We should jam!" He nodded. It was at that moment, before either of us had even made a sound, that a band was formed and a plan for world domination via rock and roll was hatched in our heads. A plan that, unfortunately, relied on our ability to get a ride to each other's houses. Teenage bands have many hurdles to overcome—paramount is that of getting a ride. Gigs, sound, songs, and talent were all secondary to getting a ride. Many a great band have been destroyed by shitty transportation. Now, most musicians are either perpetual children or horrible leeches. Before I became the latter, I was the former, as was Johnny. So, we each engaged in a timeless rock star ritual, wherein we both begged our mothers to agree to a sleepover. Since hauling drum sets are a pain in the ass, it was agreed that

I would have the opportunity to stay over at Crack Rock Johnny's house first.

Johnny lived near the old GE factory in Warren, in a part of town where blue-collar guys once raised families when the factory was still operational. Now it served as a sanctuary for crack heads and target practice for children with rocks. His house was a solid three stories and was once, I assume, quite a looker. Now, in the shadow of the empty factory, they weathered the cruel winters, losing patches of the lead paint that coated the rotting wood. At least Crack Rock Johnny's house wasn't alone. The rest of the neighborhood looked just the same. Houses in that area of Ohio used to be solid family homes that were held for generations. Just looking down the block, you could *feel* the history. The old brick street shone through the potholes that dotted the neighborhood. Old buckeye trees towered over houses with no shingles and tarps over the windows.

Johnny's family was one of the last families left standing on that side of town, which was perfect because it was a perfect place to have a band. We could play well into the night and nobody would call the cops on us. Shit, even if they did, everybody knows the cops don't go to that side of town, and even if they did, they weren't going to bother a bunch of crazy Mormons. Outside on their sagging porch was an old couch that smelled of petrochemicals and was speckled with cigarette burns. I looked at Johnny, pointed to the cigarette burns, and gave a gasp of mock shock.

"Are you serious?" he said, glaring at me.

"Yeah, now I can't be in a band with you," I laughed. "Rock stars don't smoke!"

"Well, rock stars don't carry their own shit either, but here we are," Johnny said as he kicked open his front door.

I was bum-rushed by a torrent of smells, punching and stomping my olfactory receptor and knocking it out for the count. It was like walking into a carnival where the overarching theme smell was cat piss. Luckily, the stench of menthol cigarettes and bacon grease evened out the sourness of the piss, so it was somewhat bearable. We stepped around the mounds of dirty laundry and broken baby dolls and pushed our way up the stairs. I remember thinking to myself, *what's with all the broken baby dolls? One is fine, two is fine, but there was like nine or so. What sick maniac kept giving these children babies?* See, Johnny was far from the only child in this family. His family was white trash and Mormon, and all told they had seven children. Honestly, one can't really know *exactly* how many children were in that house because, well, it was like a carnival. The number of animals was unknown to the family, I know that much. At one point, they had a raccoon living in the walls that they had named Simon, till one day there was a weird smell and everyone assumed that Simon had gone home to Jesus. Why they even had doors on the house is beyond me.

The second floor was just as confusing with the exception of one room—Johnny's sisters' room. Their room was kept immaculate. As we passed their room, his sisters, who were around my age, gave me miserable looks, which I returned. Truth be told, I had a crush on both of them, but it is imperative in rock and roll to choose the side of your bandmates, whatever the cost. I would later write a song about them and perform it with Johnny. He never suspected a thing. Problem was, neither did his sisters, so it was a dud. I had yet to learn an important truth about rock and roll: it is not the arena for subtlety. *One must be like hammer and not like breeze.* We crawled up into the attic where Johnny lived. Well, lived might be too strong a word. He *survived* up there. It was an unfinished attic, meaning no windows, no insulation, no heat in the winter, and all electricity came from an overloaded extension cord. The space reeked of stale dirty laundry and melted plastic. *This is what independence looks like*, I thought.

I set my gear down on the floor next to Johnny's mattress and popped open my case. Inside was Tracy, my first bass guitar, named after the song by Jaco Pastorius. It was plastered with stickers and pictures from magazines glued to the pickguard. Dents and love marks told the long, sordid history of my beloved bass, and I cherished each one. I unplugged his alarm clock from the extension cord, plugged in my amp, and stood poised to rock. Johnny hopped behind his drum set— an old Ludwig set from the 60s that sounded like doom. *This was it! This was the beginning of a band!*

"Let's jam!" I said with all the excitement and promise that youth affords. He clicked four with his sticks. I came down with a mighty thumping thumb on my bass and...the power in the attic went out with a pop! Apparently, when one plugs in a massive bass guitar amp into an already overloaded extension cord, it tends to trip the breaker and knock out power in the entire house. Johnny's sisters were mid-hair crimp and cursed at our rock and roll nonsense. *That's rock and roll, folks!* After a brief interruption, we eventually got the right ratio of appliances to power cords as to not overload the breaker and had a proper jam. Was it good? No, but when has that ever mattered? Music doesn't have to be good or mean anything to be worthwhile. All it has to do is move you. That's it. At that moment, for the two of us, we weren't freaks. The faces of the others in the hallway at church, in seminary class, and in every priesthood meeting eyeballing our shaggy hair were gone. For the first time, we were clear. *No sin, no expectations, no heaven, no hell, just music.* Music is a language for those who don't know the right words. It was liberating.

Unfortunately, Johnny's sisters didn't understand this and came up to tell us how bad we sucked. Their blind rage and half-crimped hair made my heart jump. *Such disheveled beauties!* I did my best to pose and look cool with my bass as they berated Johnny and I about our obnoxious noise. As they left, I felt a little betrayed by my rock star idols. *I thought being in a band would get me chicks? What the fuck? Gene Simmons, YOU LIED TO ME!*

We went outside to take a breather on the petrochemical-infused couch and to contemplate our plan to take over the music scene of Northeast Ohio. Under the hum of the ghetto streetlights, we sat kicking around band names when a car pulled into the driveway. Another station wagon, another piece of shit. I remarked at how low the car was riding and it was soon revealed to me why the car was sitting so low. The door opened and a massive figure exited the car. He was the size and build of a refrigerator and was covered only by a grey undershirt. He chomped on a cigar with his gnarled teeth. On his thick neck sat a massive head, on the side of which was a tattoo of a mosquito. It was all topped off with a bright blue Mohawk. He turned to us and looked us up and down. He crunched his way up the cracked driveway, keeping his murderous gaze fixed on me. The stairs creaked and groaned under his Doc Martins as he came directly for me. I shrunk down into the chemical smell of the couch and smiled weakly.

"This the guitar player?" he asked as he looked me over.

"Bass guitar, actually," I corrected him.

He shot me a look of crazed menace. "Bass? It's the same as guitar." I shook my head. He parked his great ugly mug right in front of mine. The stench of the cheap cigar made me queasy. "Tell me then, what's the difference?"

I sat up, gaining my confidence. If there was one thing I knew, it was what the bass could do and what it was good for.

"The difference between guitar and bass guitar," I started, "is that guitar players can *play* funk, but bass players *are* funk!"

The giant eyed me curiously then turned to Johnny. He turned back to me, cracked the widest smile, and let out a roar of laughter.

"Ok," he said, shaking my hand. "He's a real bass player. Only a bass player talks like that! Nobody else would give a shit. Nice to meet you." I watched as the Blue Mohawk entered into the house, sneaked up on Johnny's mom, and gave her a big boisterous hug.

Johnny smiled and tapped my shoulder. "That's Dad."

The Blue Mohawk was a DJ for the local classic rock station, the legendary CD 93.3: *THE WOLF!* His claim to fame (other than the blue Mohawk and the head tattoo) was the fact that during his tenure as rock n' roll DJ, he once broke into the Warren City Jail dressed as Santa Claus. When the guards were finally able to catch him, they found that instead of choo-choo trains and toys, Santa was passing out stacks of nudie magazines and cartons of Newports to all the inmates. Needless to say, that kind of made him a local hero. It also explained a lot about Johnny and why he was the way that he was. As a side gig, he DJ'd the local dive bars on the weekends. In between tracks by Tom Petty and The Rolling Stones, he'd tell dirty jokes, try to get the locals to take their clothes off, and try to stop the bar fights by blasting "Why Can't We Be Friends?" He knew a lot about music (*good* music) and I was floored that, through all that, he still considered himself Mormon. However, like my dad, the Blue Mohawk rarely went to church. It didn't matter. His family adored him.

Johnny's mom clapped her hands thrice and all of her children seemed to appear in the dining room as if summoned by magic. There was a calm immediate order over all of the inhabitants of the house. Though there was chaos in the surroundings, everyone knew their place at the table. Johnny's mom was the kind of lady who had shit locked down. She was a tough lady who was fair. It was a wonder how she managed to stay alive with as many kids as she had. I watched as she ladled out the dinner to the kids, taking time to maintain order amongst the youngest of the brood. She was in her 40s, but her eyes looked so much older. She finally sat down and scraped what little was left in the dish out for herself.

Mormonism is a patriarchal religion. Well, most religions and institutions are patriarchal, but Mormonism is pretty strict about it and is pretty resistant to change. For instance, I learned in my Sunday school lessons that men are to provide, women are to give birth and raise kids, and no one is to question this arrangement. It is doctrinal, final, absolute. It is also tragic. It's not uncommon for intelligent, ambitious women to choose having a family instead of the pursuit of their own ambitions. That's not to say that having a family is less important or rewarding than individual goals. However, in the church, there is a certain amount of pressure for women to be docile and at home. Men don't even have to make that choice. Now, if that is your choice, then that's that. The problem is not the choice, but the indoctrination of children into thinking that one choice is right and one choice is wrong. You are expected to bring as many children into the world as you are able to. Now, imagine trying to have an ambitious career with 15 kids and no help from the hubby. That might be a little difficult.

It puts pressure on both parents. It's not uncommon to hear women in the church report feeling overwhelmed with family work. Their circle of friends shrinks to who they see at church. Men get off easier, but we still have heavy expectations. For us, we are under immense pressure to succeed at careers that cut into valuable time with the family. Imagine working 50 hours a week, trying to fit in time for all eight of your kids and wife. Add on top of that the immense workload that the church puts on its members through callings and other enterprises and you can start to understand why there are so many depressed people in this religion. In the end, like in Vegas, the only winner is the house. The church gets your work for free, 10% of your cash, and the souls of your children.

During dinner, I did my best to make discreet flirty eyes to Johnny's sisters. I winked and raised my eyebrows, mixed in my geeky smolder, clicked and licked my lips, and tried every other idiot male trick in the book. Finally, the older of the two said, "Is there something stuck in your eye? What's wrong with you?" Instead of coming across as Romeo, I was coming across as Richard III. *My kingdom for a decent pick-up line.*

Thankfully, Johnny's mom put me out of my misery and changed the subject. "Hey, Alan, was it you that let Johnny borrow that CD?"

"Which one was that?" A pageant of albums with parental advisory stickers skipped merrily through my mind as I wondered how much trouble I was in.

She shook her head. "I don't know the name of it, but it had sort of a weird cover."

"Gee, *that* narrows it down," quipped the younger of the sisters.

"It was all covered in mountains, I think. Radio...something," Johnny's mom concluded. I racked my brain. Album cover? Covered in mountains? Kid tested; mother approved?

"Kid A by Radiohead? Is that the one?" I asked.

"I think so," she responded as she wiped the applesauce off the chin of her youngest son. "Yeah, I really liked that one."

Johnny's sisters looked over in surprise. "Wait, you mean to tell me that someone capable of making all that noise is also capable of having good taste in music?" they asked.

"Music that does not stir is as good as wallpaper," I said as I reattempted my flirty eyes.

"Wow, that's...so bad," muttered Johnny.

"It's really good music," responded Johnny's mom. "There are some really beautiful songs on that CD. It reminded me of when I was a girl in Iowa." *Curious.* At the time, that album was pretty groundbreaking stuff. It was, in a sense, the sound of music yet to come. Yet, here was a woman in her 40s, talking about the nostalgia that it produced.

"There was a field by my house where I used to go out and lay in the grass," she continued. "It was quiet. Peaceful." Her eyes glazed over and I could tell that she was back in that memory. Perhaps it was one she went to often. I didn't know what particular song triggered that for her and I guess it doesn't matter. What matters is that, for a moment, that music transported her to a good place. A place where there was no house full of kids, where she might have had a different life. A past that was 600 miles away. I had always wanted to make music *that* good, something that could take somebody someplace. However, time, booze, and life had other plans for me. I didn't think about it then, but I think about it now how Mormon women have their paths chosen for them. Doctrine dictates that their purpose is to be mothers and raise families. Motherhood is a blessing and a burden, but most of all, it is an identity. You are defined by your ability to have a family. Now, I love my son and my wife, but I was never told that it would define me as a person. I had a choice to be a parent. It was never my destiny, my stated purpose to bear children.

The dinner was broken by the sound of the youngest boy having a crying fit over the mashed potatoes. The Blue Mohawk stood up, slapped his belly, and gave a great groan of approval. Dinner was a success. Apparently, the family was waiting for this sign because the table became a buzz with the cleaning and stacking of plates. It was at that moment that Johnny motioned for me to follow him upstairs for a discreet exit. I smiled kindly at Johnny's sisters to which they replied with soft smiles of their own. *What a difference a Radiohead album makes!*

Johnny flipped on his radio and we spent the night debating who the best drummer was and how long guitar solos should be to be considered "epic". Though we never came to a consensus on these most delicate of issues, we were able to come to an agreement—I really needed to stop flirting with Johnny's sisters. *C'est la vie.* By the time we finally drifted off into dreams of Rockstar domination, it was almost dawn. I dreamt of Johnny and I on a stage somewhere, a crowd of faceless fanatics chanting for our music. Johnny's sisters blew me kisses from the corner of the stage while the Blue Mohawk threw people around in the mosh pit. I was singing a song about a woman in Iowa and how peace is there whenever she closes her eyes.

Chapter 10

For the "Strength" of Our Youth

Many moons ago, when Jnco's and frosted tips were all the rage, Crack Rock Johnny and I attended a Stake dance. It was lucky for us that it was a Stake dance and not a Ward dance because, well, we were enormous fuck-ups. No girl in her right mind who had seen our shenanigans would permit us a dance…or so I thought. With the benefit of hindsight, I am able to see a little clearer what was going on and what it all meant. Maybe it meant nothing, I don't know. All I know is that what was happing for teens back then is still happening now, and that is really not good. Admittedly, this sounds cryptic and apocalyptic, but I think it will become clearer as I go along. I hope.

Anyway, between requesting that the DJ play Korn and Limp Bizkit and trying desperately to get a mosh pit started, Johnny and I were put on notice from the church Elders. The exchange went something like this:

>**Elder 1**: Hey, I know you two are here to have a little bit of fun and cut loose. I think everyone can appreciate that. However, would you mind not being so unruly?
>
>**Me**: Huh?
>
>**Crack Rock Johnny**: Dude, I think he wants us to calm down.
>
>**Me**: What do you mean?
>
>**Elder 1**: Yeah, if you could stop with the smash pit, that would be great.
>
>**Me** (to Crack Rock Johnny): Is this guy real or are the drugs you gave me finally kicking in?

As the night went on and our attempts at more "smash pits" were thwarted, we changed our approach. We thought that since it was, in fact, a dance, perhaps we might want to try to do a bit of actual dancing. I use the term "dancing" very loosely because, well, I'm whiter than a glass of milk on a paper plate in a snowstorm. Let's just say that I gave it my best shot. Johnny was significantly more handsome than me, so the girls were more than eager to dance with him, despite his conspicuous idiocy. Within a couple of minutes, I found myself alone, mulling about the fringes of the dancefloor, looking for a good place to stand and fade into obscurity.

Standing alone by the wall, I assessed my situation with some anxiety. It sucks to be a teenager and it sucks even worse when you come to the realization that you are responsible for whether or not you are alone in life. It's a heavy existential crisis to have at a "fun" dance. I suppose that's why everyone is so focused on "looking right" and saying the "right thing", not only as a teenager but as an adult as well. It's a lovely distraction from the fact that, eventually, we are all alone. Further along the wall was Ms. Overbite in a seemingly similar predicament. Perhaps she too was contemplating the existential horror of the futility of this moment in our lives. Perhaps she was deconstructing the preconceived roles of the woman in the nuclear family. Perhaps, just maybe, she wanted to dance with somebody. *Yeah, I'll roll the dice on that one,* I thought. I knew that she hated me and I figured that it would be a horrendous crash and burn, but I slunk over to her nonetheless. Frankly, I was surprised that no one had asked her to dance. I'd always had a crush on her, but seeing as how I acted like an idiot most of the time, I didn't expect her to feel the same way.

"Hey there," I said with some apprehension.

"Hey," she responded dryly, her eyes fixed to the floor. She was swaying in time with the music.

"Do you like this music?" I asked, a little surprised.

"I do," she said dismissively. "Are you gonna make fun of me for it?"

"Not at all," I said earnestly. It was Dave Matthews singing 'Crash Into Me', a song that should probably not be played at a dance full of sexually repressed teenagers, but whatever. *Rock on, DMB!*

"Would it ruin your enjoyment of the music if you were dancing with me?" I asked. She gave me a curious appraisal and shook her head, though not without some apprehension. I held out my hand and she took it.

We nestled into the midst of the Mormon mêlée, all of us keeping a conspicuous space between us and our partners, all of us doing the awkward teenage sway that passed for slow dancing. I could feel the tension in her arms as they draped stiffly around my neck. I smiled earnestly and did my best to set her at ease. She eyed me suspiciously. To be fair, if *I* had asked *me* to dance, *I* would have been suspicious too. Luckily, the silence was brief. Unluckily, it was not to my benefit.

"Why did you ask me to dance?" asked Ms. Overbite.

"Well, I…really…like this song," I stammered.

"Sure," she nodded facetiously.

"No, I'm serious. Actually, I'm surprised you know this song."

"Why? It's on *every* radio station and in *every* store at the mall."

I nodded. "Yeah, it is. I guess I'm surprised because, well, it's not exactly rated PG, is it?"

"What do you mean?" she asked suspiciously. Dave Matthews answered her question by asking his girl to hike up her skirt a little more. Her face blushed.

"Good song, no?" I smiled.

Annoyed, she asked, "Why did you really ask me to dance?"

"Because I wanted to," I responded sincerely.

"Ok," she scoffed.

"Well, why did you say yes?" I asked defensively.

"Because we are supposed to," she retorted.

I didn't know it at the time, but the girls were told that if a boy asked them to dance, they should say yes, even if they didn't want to. The reason behind it was that it takes courage to ask someone to dance and none to refuse. How bad can it be to dance with someone for three minutes? How bad can it be to do something that you absolutely do not want to do for three minutes? It's a philosophy that lays the groundwork for women to be compliant victims, unable to use their voice when something is happening to them that they don't like. It teaches them that men's feelings are the only ones worth considering. If you refuse, you are the bad guy. Knowing this information now makes me feel dirty, like I took something from somebody. An unknown violation in the presence of how many others?

The church laid the groundwork for this a few weeks before the dance. The Sunday before, we were given a pamphlet called 'For the Strength of Our Youth'. Essentially, it's a piece of Mormon etiquette, designed to squash healthy exploration and boundaries, and to create a sense of guilt and shame about one's bodies and desires. It also serves to indoctrinate Mormon kids at an early age to strive for a level of "morality" and perfection that can never realistically be achieved. Music, language, dress, dating, and dancing were all rigidly laid out and directed for us. These seem trivial the older we get, but in our youth, appearance is everything. There is safety in classification. As a teenager, we defined ourselves by the clothes we wore, our hair color, our friends, and most importantly, our music. In the church, identity was something to be assigned to us, not to be searched for. Discovery was a dangerous word. These realizations would come later in life, accompanied by some heavy guilt and a desire to begin reprogramming myself. However, that night at the dance, it was just me and Ms. Overbite, swaying out of time to the music.

"Are you doing this to make fun of me?" she blurted out. We stopped our swaying.

"What?"

"I know you and Johnny are weirdos and I don't know what you are trying to do. I don't want to end up a punch line."

"Actually," I said in measured calm, "I have been wanting to get to know you for quite some time, but I guess you've always been too good to talk to me. This dance is kind of a big deal for me."

"Really?" she responded kindly. I could feel the tension start to ease. "You know, if you didn't act so ridiculous, I might talk to you. Did you ever think of that?"

"Obviously not," I sighed. "In any case, it's a moot point."

"I suppose it is," she said. The song ended. I thanked her for the dance and watched as she melted back into the group of her friends. I spied Johnny across the room making progress with a blonde who had scandalously visible shoulders. I figured he didn't need me gumming up the works, so I stepped outside for a smoke n' stroll. Like most addicts, it was around this age that I started "experimenting" with drugs and alcohol. I'd always thought that term was stupid. It wasn't an *experiment* for me. I knew what would happen if I smoked and drank—I would be like Mom and Dad. Simple. What *wasn't* so simple was how to get my smokes, especially when I was as broke as a joke and I didn't have any friends who were old enough to buy them. So, like any teenage scumbag, I stole them from my parents. About a block away from the church, I popped in a smoke and lit up. That good old teenage depression was setting in like a frost.

I rolled Ms. Overbite's words around in my head and let them mix with the cigarette smoke. *"You know, if you didn't act so ridiculous, I might talk to you. Did you ever think of that?"* I exhaled both the words and the smoke through pursed lips and stomped the purloined cigarette out on the cracked blacktop. *Put those thoughts out of your head. Don't let them find purchase.* I think that a lot of what was happening for me in the church was working its way into my secular life. I had to face the fact that I was wearing a mask and I didn't like myself. I saw no future. *Change the way I act? For what? Why would I want what that would bring?* I didn't want that life. To be frank, I didn't want *any* life at that point. I didn't feel it was worth it. Still, I envisioned a normal life, swaying to music with a dance partner who *wanted* to dance. A deep part of me soared at the prospect. It would be a while before it came out in proper.

That was the last time I had gone to a church dance. The shenanigans that Johnny and I were famous for took a back seat more and more those days. Our friendship was changing. Growing up will do that. Time and space are wonderful and terrible things. If you give yourself enough time and space, it's amazing what you'll see. Recently, I came across Ms. Overbite on social media and I took a look at how she was doing. She was wearing a BYU hoodie surrounded by kids. She looked happy and I hope she is. Everyone has a right to be happy, and nobody—not even the mighty Mormon Church—has a right to trample on that.

Chapter 11

The Accidental Bare-Assed Water-Skiing Incident

Like most Mormon boys, I was attached to the scouting program from a young age. Scouting is one of the only good things that I associate with the church. I got to go camping in some really interesting places and was able to see some really impressive natural wonders. The scouts have become a magnet for controversy in recent years, with scandals and allegations of abuse. I was lucky in the fact that I never experienced any of that, and I feel so rotten that there are evil fuckers who would take that program and pervert it the way they did.

Anyway, back when I was a teenager, my troop decided to take all of us out to the lake to do some waterskiing. Ohio is full of lakes and most of them suck, but this one allowed waterskiing, so that was that.

One of the dads in our troop just had a massive payday on a horse race and he plopped his winnings down on a badass motorboat. This thing was sweet. It had all sorts of shiny shit that sparkled and rumbled when gassed up. It had a killer sound system that seemed incapable of playing anything other than Ted Nugent and Whitesnake. Best of all, it had the most metal name in all of boat-hood. It was called 'The Eager Wench' and it had a picture of a buxom pirate girl on the hood. Betwixt her shapely legs was a treasure chest full of brewskis. Needless to say, this guy was not a Mormon.

Nor was his boy, which is probably why I got along with him so well. He was an outsider amongst our mostly Mormon troop, so we called him NoMo. He knew that Crack Rock Johnny and myself were weirdoes, so I think he gave us a pass. Whenever we would have to pray before a troop meeting, NoMo would roll his eyes along with Johnny and myself and make faces at us, trying to get us to bust out. We would usually share a tent during camping trips, keeping each other up with dirty jokes and listening to stoner metal on our cassettes. For those of you who don't know what a cassette is, well, ask your grandpa.

The morning of the waterskiing trip was gray and humid—a typical August morning in Ohio. We got up at the ass-crack of dawn and met over at the church, piled into Brother Mooreman's Econoline bus, and set off toward the lake. Johnny, NoMo, and I took the backseat and passed the time by playing air guitar and air drums to Rush. We were halfway through 'YYZ' when we pulled into a McDonald's for breakfast. *Shit*, I thought, *I forgot to bring more than a couple bucks*. Eh, a couple bucks was enough for a cup of coffee, and that was enough for me.

At that particular moment, I felt groggy, shitty, and decided that I needed a pick-me-up. Though my family had trained me to keep my breaking of the Word of Wisdom hidden, my internal needs won out. 'Twas coffee I wanted, so coffee I must have! I went up to the counter, threw my crumpled ones at the surly fellow operating the register, and got my coffee. Before I even had it to my lips, the voice of Brother Mooreman jolted me out of my quiet, reflective pleasure.

"Brother Young, may I ask what is in that cup?" he said with the same booming authority he used when bearing his testimony on Sundays.

"You may ask," I replied.

He frowned. "I assume that is hot chocolate. If so, I would like to have a sip."

That's weird, I thought. *Who demands a sip of someone else's drink at a McDonald's? Bitch, get your own!* Now, part of me wanted to let this guy go for it and have his first taste of coffee. I wanted to see the realization flood his face that he had tasted the devil's brew. I wanted to see him rend his garments in agony, twist on the floor in anguish that he allowed himself the beautiful and bitter black brew that McDonald's sold to me. That would have been hilarious, but not cool on my part. I'm not that big of a dick.

"Actually, it's coffee," I broke it to him. "I don't think you would like it."

"Coffee?" he asked. "Obviously they made a mistake."

"No, it's coffee for a reason."

He scoffed. "What's the reason?"

I was up all night watching satanic gay porn and cutting myself with a Black Sabbath CD. This will be the final, delicious step in my transformation into full demon.

"I'm tired and I need a boost," I responded with finality. I knew that he knew about my family being the way they were and I was in no mood to get shit on because of it. I was done talking and I wanted to sip my coffee.

"We should meet with the bishop," he said. "I am worried about you. I don't want you getting addicted to coffee."

"Ok, sounds good," I said dismissively as I made my way back to Crack Rock Johnny and NoMo.

"Dude, what was that about?" asked NoMo.

"He was freaking out about the coffee."

"Dude, you got coffee?" asked Johnny. "You know he's going to tell your mom."

"Yeah, I'm sure it will tear her apart," I said with a coy smile. "'My boy! A coffee drinker? Motherfucker! I'll chop his dick off for this!' Get real!" Johnny nodded in understanding.

NoMo looked at us curiously. "What *is* the coffee thing about? I mean, I get the polygamy and the no dancing, but what's up with the coffee?" Johnny and I laughed. NoMo knew the Mormon stereotypes, so he was more than willing to bust our balls every now and again.

"First off, Mormons are allowed to dance," I corrected him. "It's just that we are horrible at it."

"Yeah, and if you make fun of polygamy again, I'll have all six of my moms come and kick your ass!" Johnny added with a stony seriousness.

"Fair enough," NoMo giggled uncomfortably. "But seriously, what is up with the coffee?" Johnny and I gave each other a mischievous smile. Fucking with people was a hobby that he and I both enjoyed, so I stepped back and followed his lead.

"Well," Johnny started, "it all started years ago when the church was formed."

"Yeah," I continued, "Joseph Smith was up one night translating the Book of Mormon and he was getting a little tired and needed a pick-me-up. Satan knew that Joseph had a predilection for the smooth brew of Columbian beans, so he hid himself in a pouch of beans from Bogota."

Johnny smiled and took over. "When Joseph Smith opened the bag of coffee, the devil popped out and started punching him in his face! Joseph was strong, though."

"Oh, man, was he!" I exclaimed. "He beat the piss out of him and was like 'Be gone, Motherfucker!' Satan left, but before he did, he cursed every coffee bean on the planet. True story!"

"If you drink too much of it, you get possessed by the devil. That's why coffee is a black liquid—because it's pure evil," concluded Johnny.

"And pure delicious!" I said as I took a long, generous swig of my coffee. NoMo scoffed and turned to me. All of a sudden, my hands started shaking and I rolled my eyes back into my head. I started talking in tongues. Johnny began muttering a compilation of prayers from *The Omen* and *The Exorcist*. NoMo stepped back a good ten feet before he realized we were messing with him.

"You guys suck! I'm gonna get you for that!" NoMo said as he made his way back to the van. Unbeknownst to me, his revenge would be swift and mighty.

The sky had cleared from its dreary grey to an almost blue when we arrived at the lake. NoMo's dad was putting 'The Eager Wench' into the water, sending water rippling up the side, over the portrait of the pirate lass.

He looked over to NoMo, Johnny, and myself, winked, and said, "I know how to get 'em wet, don't I?" We all gave an uncomfortable laugh and cringed. NoMo's dad slid his can of Milwaukee's Best into a beer cozy that read 'I love my girlfriend, but don't tell my wife!'

Apparently, we were not the only ones who were going to take advantage of this rarest of sunny days because the lake was pretty crowded. Two elderly men in the middle of the lake were rowing about in a canoe that had been duct-taped to hell. Across the lake, there was a family of seven listening to Lynyrd Skynyrd and waving Confederate flags. Just then, a blue flash of light caught my attention. A loud roar followed, like a tiny child trying to keep up with its brother. A boat full of impossibly gorgeous, impossibly blonde girls in bikinis waved at the lot of us awkward scouts waiting to hop into 'The Eager Wench'. They flew past again, honking at us and blowing kisses, watching us all trying to suck in our guts and flex our non-existent muscles. Not much has changed for me, I'm afraid.

We all aggressively pushed into the boat, trying to project our masculinity in case the blondes came back. Men become insanely aggressive with each other in the presence of pretty women. I remember once I punched a kid in the hallway at school because a girl that I liked waved at him instead of me. I also remember that the kid kicked me in the nuts as a retaliation, and we both got in trouble. Likewise, I envisioned throwing Johnny and NoMo out of the goddamn boat if I had to in order to have a shot with these blondes. Masculinity is a bitch sometimes. Luckily for us, NoMo's dad was about to take care of that issue because each of us was given a bright purple life vest. Each of us complained in our own unique way as we snapped these horrific monstrosities on. Now we looked like a boat full of adolescent Barneys. I thought, *serves us right for being such dicks!* The boat roared into life and NoMo's dad set off after the boatload of buxom blonde beauties.

Johnny jumped into his ritual of flipping his hair about, trying to make it picture-perfect for the ladies, only to have his efforts thwarted by the rushing wind. NoMo was scratching the tartar off his teeth with his fingernail and wiping it onto his swim trunks. As for me, well, I was lamenting my fashion choices. I had on a pair of cotton shorts that were cinched up with a threadbare waist-string. Granted, it was not exactly 'high fashion', but it was all I had. I had asked my mom to take me to get new trunks, but she insisted that these tattered trunks were sufficient. Anyway, like everyone else, I was commando under the shorts because, well, guys don't swim with underwear on. It's weird. Seriously, ask *any* guy.

We arrived at a spot in the middle of the lake that was open and calm and NoMo's dad went over the basics of waterskiing. He told us to hold onto the rope, plant our feet, and try to stay on balance. *Try to stay on balance? How hard could it be? You're just standing there, essentially.* I figured if Marty McFly could hang onto a car while he was skateboarding, I could hold onto a speeding boat while wearing skis. Being young and stupid has its advantages. NoMo was first up. Since he had a lot of experience, he took time to show us how to hold onto the rope, how to stand slowly and balance correctly, and what to do in case we fell over into the water. *Does he not understand that I have seen Back to the Future 68 times? I got this!* I stared out across the water, watching the boat of blondes speeding by. My mind floated into fantasy, where a scene was creating itself. Ladies and gentlemen, the *Waterskiing Fantasy in E Major.*

The picture bloomed before me. I would wait eagerly for the boat to take off, gripping the rope with stoic determination. The boat would launch, I would rise gracefully to my feet, and I would be waterskiing. The blonde beauties would pull up alongside the speeding boat and marvel at my prowess. I would flex my incredible muscles, tearing apart the lifejacket, and making the girls swoon with my physique. Naturally, I would be doing all sorts of awesome flips. Maybe someone would toss me an old Jazzmaster and I could do a killer surf rock riff. Why not! Inevitably, one of the blondes would faint, fall into the water, require me to save her, and we would fall in love and grow old together. Every good fantasy needs a moral center. As I sat, humming the wedding march, the boat slowed to a stop and NoMo pulled himself back into the boat.

"Dude, did you see that gnarly jump I did? I almost killed myself with that!" NoMo laughed.

"Yeah, you are crazy, man!" I lied. *A jump almost killed him? Man, I'll show you how to do it in just a moment. Gonna shred on 'Miserlou' too.* He obviously didn't live in the same headspace I did.

"It's cool," Johnny said. "I got a picture of it, I think."

"Sweet," said NoMo. "We'll make sure to get a picture of you if you make it up."

"*If?*" scoffed Johnny. "What do you mean '*if*'?"

"Dude, I just got good at this like a week ago and I've been doing it way longer than you guys have. It's hard."

"Speaking of hard, when do you think the blondes are coming back?" I asked. Brother Mooreman flashed me a dirty look.

Johnny was next up. He bobbed in the water for a minute as his purple lifejacket fought against the water and tried to decapitate him. By this time, the boatload of blondes was back to watch the show. Johnny flipped his hair one last time before the Eager Wench roared to life and he was jerked into action. His hands clenched desperately onto the rope. His face fought the stinging water. He mouthed a series of obscenities that only NoMo and myself even dared to decipher.

"Dude, I think he's gonna try to stand up!" I called to NoMo over the titanic sound of the engine. "Get ready with the camera!"

Johnny started up slowly, pushing himself up gently on the advice of NoMo. A smile came over his face when he was halfway up. There was a round of applause from the boat of blondes. Upon hearing this, Johnny shot up too eagerly, either to impress the girls or out of shock. The front of his water-skis caught the water, sending Johnny front-flipping ass over tits into the air and finally crashing into the lake.

"I-I think I got him mid-flip," giggled NoMo.

"That was the most beautiful thing I've ever seen," I said in astonishment, fighting back tears of laughter. "I'd never seen anyone flip over that many times."

"I did," answered Brother Mooreman. "Once, in a Romanian circus on my mission. Flexible people, the Romanians."

Johnny emerged, coughing up what he had swallowed of the lake, and desperately trying to fix his hair so that it was presentable. The blondes applauded his attempt and blew him consolatory kisses. Johnny's red face was partially disguised by the purple shade of the life vest. All of us on The Eager Wench laughed and applauded Johnny as he pushed himself back into the boat. He smiled over at the boat full of blondes, who waved at him.

"Dude, they're only waving at you because they are being sympathetic," said NoMo.

"Hey, there is a fine line between getting *sympathy* and getting *laid,* and I intend to cross it," replied Johnny. He turned to me and asked, "What are you waiting for? Maybe you'll get some sympathy too."

I looked over toward the blondes, gave them a confident wink, and turned back to Johnny and NoMo. "I don't *need* sympathy. I only need space to do my thang!"

"You've never been whiter than at this moment," said Johnny as he clapped my back.

I plunged into the lake with the skis on. The cold water instantly flooded the space between my life vest and my skin, surrounding me and shrinking and clenching every protrusion and orifice on my body. *It's ok,* I thought, *none of that is visible, so it doesn't matter.* The only thing that I had intended to be visible was my incredible waterskiing ability and my rippling muscles, which I assumed would develop sometime in the next five to ten seconds. I gripped the rope with my hands. I planted my feet under my body. The tips of the skis bobbed gently out of the water and I gave the thumbs up to Johnny and NoMo. The boat rumbled to life. The rope tightened along with my grip. This was it. This was my time to shine!

The boat took off at incredible speed, yanking my body forward and sending me face-down into the water. The once enveloping water had turned into hard concrete. The water-skis dragged under the water, keeping me from being able to rise up as the water slapped across my face, forcing its way into my mouth, over my tongue, and down my throat. Luckily, I didn't have time to taste what was going into my stomach. I could hear Jonny and NoMo shouting words of encouragement over the laughter of the others. I could hear the boatload of blondes urging me on as well. This was it. The fantasy I had envisioned with its glorious moral center was washed away in a torrent of stinging mist and lake scum. There was no way that my embarrassment could get any worse.

Or was there?

At that moment, I felt the skis liberate themselves from my feet and land somewhere in the murky depths behind me. I held onto the rope with my dear life. The water tried desperately to make me part with the rope, pulling my body, throwing it from side to side over the wake of the boat. To my horror, I realized that my body wasn't the only thing that the water was pulling and clawing away at. The threadbare waist string that held up my cotton shorts had been putting up a good fight against the forces of the rushing water. Alas, like Beauregard at Shiloh, it couldn't hold up to superior force and it snapped. I felt the shorts being tugged away from my body. I clenched every muscle I could, hoping to catch a strip or a wrinkle of fabric between some cheek or fold in my body. No good. The shorts pulled farther and farther down my body till I felt a curious sensation on my ass—a warm, light, and airy sensation. It was seeing the sunshine for the first time in its life. It's a freeing sensation in a way, to be dragged through the water bare-assed, the world shining its light and warmth down on the most hidden of hidden. It was almost enough to distract me from the fact that my shorts had officially parted ways with my body and were now airborne. Gravity eventually took over, sending my threadbare shorts floating gently down to the surface of the lake.

My fingers clung desperately to the rope as the waves tossed my body around. A particularly nasty wave ended what little time I had on the line, officially putting me out of my bare-assed misery. I was later told that the eternity I thought I spent on that rope was only about 40 seconds. However, it was more than enough time to expose my bare-ass, twig and berries, and my waterskiing ineptitude to my scout troop and the boatload of blondes. I bobbed in the water, hearing the roars of laughter from the guys on the boat and the shrill giggles of the ladies not far away. I pleaded with my life vest to malfunction in some way so that I could drown and put myself out of the misery of this unkind world. To my chagrin, it held firm.

"That was awesome!" cried Johnny. NoMo was speechless. Tears were rolling down his face as he tried to breathe through his laughter. All he could do was point to his camera. *Well, his revenge was swift and just,* I thought. But it wasn't over. The laughter was interrupted by the sweetest voice I had ever heard.

"I think these belong to you," the statuesque blonde said as she tossed me my trunks. "They landed next to my Zima. Thought you might want them back."

"Yeah," said another blonde. "You don't want to be putting ideas in our heads, do you?" I tried my best to unhook the life vest and precipitate my drowning, but no luck. I smiled and gave a nod of appreciation as I slid the trunks on underwater, doing my best to ignore the rapid shutter of NoMo's camera clicking.

"Hey, man, you said you didn't want sympathy!" said Johnny.

The blondes blew us all kisses and headed off. The rest of the troops all had their turn in the lake. Some got it, some didn't, but none had the luck I did. The adventure ended when I was dropped off at home and was able to escape the hours of relentless ball-busting and shit-talking, courtesy of a scout troop of adolescent Mormons. I clapped my headphones around my ears, cranked it up, and tried to forget everything that had ever happened to me in my entire life. I fell asleep that night, glad that the embarrassment was over. Well, not completely over. Unfortunately, next Sunday when I went to church, there was a throng gathered around the bulletin board, all giggling and backslapping one another. As I made my way toward the board, I could sense the crowd trying to stifle its laughter.

That's when I saw it: a series of photos chronicling the saga of the prodigal swim trunks, courtesy of NoMo and his shitty disposable camera. Three photos in glorious Kodak color. I nodded, sighed, and went on about my day. What was the point in trying to hide them? It was known, and trying to get anything unknown in the church is a futile gesture. In many cases, it's best to numb yourself, smile, and giggle as if you are in on the joke. It doesn't make it suck any less, but at least you are able to get away from the crowds a little easier. *If the wolves can't smell blood, they won't tear you apart*, I thought.

It was the crowd that I had the issue with, not the guy snapping the pictures. With Johnny and NoMo, that photoshoot wasn't personal, it was business. The business of being a teenage dipshit. It was a perfect scenario for the best kind of ball-busting—one with visual proof. It's Man-Law. It sucks, but it's understandable. Is it any surprise why so many boys end up being maladjusted men?

****

Despite that little bit of treachery, I still stayed friends with Johnny and NoMo. They were the only cool kids I knew in that Mormon world. Unfortunately, with most cool kids, their parents get jobs out of state and they leave. It happened to NoMo, just as it happened to Johnny. Johnny's dad, the Blue Mohawk, got a job in Arizona. We tried to stay in contact, but it wasn't happening. Last I heard of him was that he was having trouble fitting in at his high school. I could relate. NoMo moved to Michigan, and as far as I know, he's still out there waterskiing and tearing up the lake, blasting Ted Nugent.

As for me, I was playing solo again. The church halls felt dangerous again. Sundays went back to being dreaded blocks on the calendar. Life in general got a lot more dangerous. It was a time when a lot changed for me. I was 16, and I started drinking a lot more. I got into many fights in school and it started to be a dangerous place. I started carrying a knife with me

195

outside and inside school. I guess I did it to feel safe, but most everyone in Ohio has a gun, so I dunno. It was a strange time. Depression was a regular guest star on the little TV show of my life. I didn't really have a lot of opportunities to work on myself. However, that didn't stop the church from reaching out to me.

One night, as I was plotting on how to snatch a pack of smokes from my parental units, I got a call from the new Bishop at the church. At that point, I hadn't gone to church in like two months and I don't really think anyone had noticed. However, this guy was all about reaching his quota. He wanted to put asses in seats! Mom called me in from the other room where I was busy trying to snatch a lighter.

"Hello?"

"Is this Alan?" asked the new bishop.

"Yep," I answered.

"*Yes*," he hissed. "It's not '*Yep*', it's '*Yes*'. How do you plan on getting ahead in life with that?"

"Um, ok," I said, immediately checking out.

"We haven't seen you at church in a while. Why is that?"

"Work," I said through a mouth full of cookies. "Gotta make pizzas for the after-church crowd."

"I see," he replied darkly. "Since you're working, I assume you're paying tithing? How much did you pay last month?"

"Nothing," I replied.

"I see." I heard him take a deep breath. "Let me tell you how it is for a young man like you—"

I cut him off. "Look, I got homework to do. Can I call you some other time?"

"How about you meet with me on Sunday? Does that work for you?"

"Yep," I said.

"*Yes*," he hissed. "Start practicing that."

"K," I replied and hung up the phone. I turned to my mom. "That guy is a total dipshit."

I snatched up a few more cookies and went back to my room. I was pissed, but I was tired. I was tired of dressing and talking and thinking like a bunch of people who I didn't like and who didn't like me, where nobody wanted me as I was. Why would anyone want to be in a place where they are not wanted? My mom had given up on trying to get me to go to church with her. I worked on Sunday mornings just to make sure I had a legit excuse. I might have hated my job, but at least my boss left me the fuck alone. That's what I wanted now from the church, to be left the fuck alone. No contact, no mention, no hassle. However, as I found out, and as Mormons are apt to lament, I could leave the church, but I couldn't leave it alone.

TALES FROM OUTER DARKNESS

Part Three
The Great Apostasy
Extravaganza!

"A good man is a good man, whether in this church or out of it." – *Brigham Young, 2nd President of the Church of Jesus Christ of Latter-day Saints*

"I have not a doubt but there will be hundreds who will leave us and go away to our enemies. I wish they would go this fall: it might relieve us from much trouble; for if men turn traitors to God and His Servants, their blood will surely be shed, or else they will be damned, and that too according to their covenants."

- Apostle Heber C. Kimball, Journal of Discourses, v. 4, p. 375

Chapter 12
Last Call

The last time that I ever set foot inside of a Mormon church was a strange affair. It had nothing to do with my resignation—that wouldn't come for another year or so after. Nor did it have anything to do with a religious service. In fact, it was on a weekday afternoon. No one of authority was there, only my mom and myself. It had nothing to do with anything Mormon-related or related to religion. It was a family issue that had been experienced but never mentioned. I had taken on the family trait, so to speak.

I grew up in a household that, by all clinical definition, was an alcoholic household. Growing up, like most alcoholic families, we weren't allowed to mention the elephant in the room. The consequences varied from chastisement to getting yelled at, and one instance of getting slapped across the face. *Addiction, man. No matter how well you think you got a hold of that tiger, you still get scratched from time to time.*

My parents made a point of noting that we were never without food or a roof over our heads. It's true, I never had to worry about any housing or food issues. Bills were paid, cars maintained, and my parents made it to their jobs on time. They were, by their own definition, "functioning alcoholics", and according to them (and our corner of Ohio), that made everything ok. Health didn't even cross our minds. Physical health didn't mean much, as long as you could get up and go to work. Mental health was a term that phycologists made up to sell prescriptions. Familial health was…well, I still don't know what that is. My parents had *outwardly* successful lives, at least better than the ones their parents did. The façade of normality was in place and it provided a sturdy wall behind which we could all participate in the weird circus that alcoholic families know too well. *Come see the show, everyone! A nice house full of miserable people!* Each person had their role and we played it out of ignorance and necessity. Simply put: we didn't know any better and we didn't know how to learn.

I don't blame my parents for this. On the contrary, they did way better than their circumstances dictated. They came from horrible, shitty situations and they managed to survive. Most of all, they managed not to commit many of the sins their parents had. I respect the hell out of them for that. Also, I understand why they used alcohol as a means to function. Sometimes the pain and anger we carry inside of us is so great that it is easier to numb it rather than deal with it. Substance abuse is rarely the cause, but almost always a symptom of something larger. However, it still left me with a hefty tab of my own to pay. Alcoholism was something that I inherited, both in my blood and in my choices. Addiction is like that. I had to reckon with their issues and ultimately had to learn how to do better than them. I suspect my son will have to learn how to do better than me. *C'est la vie.*

In any case, my family was most assuredly not in line with the *Word of Wisdom*, the half-assed commandment set down by Joseph Smith back in the day. For those who are uninitiated, the Word of Wisdom is where Mormons get the no coffee, no alcohol, no tobacco rule that everyone likes to make fun of them for. I could go into great detail about the contradictions, controversies, and conundrums that it has created, but I've used up all my energy on amazing alliterations. *That English degree just pays for itself!*

I had a theory that the reason we didn't get more shit for it was the fact that we were Youngs. We can trace our family back to the founding of the church. The way I understand it, my great-whatever grandfather was the father of Brigham Young. Pretty cool, huh? Not really. When you take into account the fucking volume of descendants from the Young family, it looks more like a roach colony in a Trumbull County trailer park. Finding a Young in a Mormon church is like finding a Mary in a Catholic one. My dad was actually invited to meet the "prophet" sometime in the 80s, but amazingly, he declined. I asked him why he declined to meet the "prophet" and he looked down at his feet, flicked the ashes from his cigarette, and shrugged. Maybe he just didn't feel like it. Maybe he didn't care. Maybe he didn't feel like he should. Fuck it, I hold my dad in higher regard than any "prophet".

By the time I graduated in 2004, I had laid the groundwork for what would become my alcoholism. I spent as much time as I could out of the house, among the ticking timebombs that were my friends. All of us had some kind of substance abuse issue. Interestingly enough, all of us also had strict religious influences. I'm not saying that a strict religious upbringing will always bring about substance abuse, but think back to when you were in high school. Chances are that the kid who sold the best pot or had the best pills probably had a mom or dad that had a Jesus fish bumper sticker.

Needless to say, whenever the church came knocking, I was nowhere to be found. Whenever the elders came by to see my mom, I made sure I had band practice. Whenever the bishop tried to get me to go on house calls with him, I was "suddenly ill". It worked most of the time. When it didn't and the church did catch up with me, I placated them as much as I could just to get them off my back. They knew that I wasn't interested and I think after a while they gave up trying.

Fine by me. I had often wondered if my alcoholism could have been dealt with if our family was somehow more involved in the church. Who's to say? Church people tend to think that more church will just about cure anything. The thing about addiction is that when you've decided to hurt yourself, to indulge and commit to that way of life, no one can stop you except yourself. In short, God didn't stand a chance in the ring with Jack Daniels.

By the age of 21, I was already a full-fledged alcoholic. I was drinking a 12-pack every night and harder stuff whenever I could swipe it out of someone's liquor cabinet. At this point in my life, I was about to be tossed out of school, my girlfriend was about to dump my ass, and I had pissed my credit so far into the ground that I couldn't even buy a pack of smokes to help the hangover pass. Unlike my parents, I was *not* a functioning alcoholic. I felt ashamed, not because of where I was, but because I couldn't drink like my parents. I felt like there was something wrong with me. There *was*, of course, something wrong with me. There was lots wrong with me. People don't drink like I did when things are going good for them. Drinking was a shitty way to cope with a life that was turning to shit. I knew all of this at the time, and despite this, I wasn't able to "control" my drinking. There's an old saying in Alcoholics Anonymous, "One is too many, and a thousand is never enough."

My mom knew that I was drinking, but she didn't know how much. Each night, my parents would bring home a 12-pack a piece and add it to the stock of beer in the fridge upstairs. It was easy to sneak as many as I wanted, adding to the stash that I had procured already. My parents unknowingly bankrolled a lot of my alcoholism. When they *did* find a few extra beer cans in the trash, they chalked it up to me having a few, but not enough to worry. You see, us addicts are smart. They only saw about *half* of what I drank. I had hiding places and disposal methods that helped hide the extent, but not the result of my drinking. I knew to give them just enough to know, but not enough to throw a fit. That was until I stopped caring if they knew.

Once I was legally allowed to buy alcohol, it was all over. I drank myself through the brown spectrum of alcohol, sticking close to the whiskeys and bourbons. I defined myself by what I drank. *No vodka for me, thanks. I'm a whiskey man! Fuck outta here with that liquid piss American beer and hand me a Guinness! If I don't piss burning fire by the end of the night, then I haven't finished drinking!* I drank, drove around, lied to the people I loved, stole from my friends and family, and fulfilled my potential of becoming a class-A scumbag. Life was like that for a time, which just so happened to be around the time I last stepped inside of a Mormon church.

It was a Thursday, I think. I had just come back to the house after making it to my last class of the day. I had steadily been declining in my attendance at Youngstown State University and was now only making it to one class. I lit up a cigarette, tossed my bag down on my bed, and went over to my desk. I knew that inside my desk was a shot or two of Canadian Club whiskey. I had work later and I knew it was going to suck as usual. Math was never my strong suit, but I could see that adding those factors meant I would benefit from a jump-start from the bottle. I slid the rusty drawer open, pushed aside an old unfinished songbook, and ran my hand across…nothing. The bottle was gone. *Where was it?* My anxiety shot through the roof. *Did I finish it last night? Was I stupid enough to not have left a little more for today? Jesus Christ, what kind of idiot doesn't have some fuel in reserve?* I turned out the remains of the draw onto the floor, scattering the ashes from my cigarette over the pictures of my ex-girlfriends. The bottle wasn't there. It *really* wasn't there. A horrifying thought popped into my head: *Did I leave it out somewhere?*

I tore through the trashcans like a crackhead raccoon, thinking that, in my drunken stupor, I might have finished it and tossed it. No luck. With a steady anxious stream of 'motherfucker' and 'cocksucker' flowing from my pursed lips, I turned to see Mom making her way toward me, hoisting the missing bottle in her left hand.

"Ah," was all I managed to get out before her hand collided with my face, sending the freshly lit cigarette pirouetting out across the driveway and into oblivion. My glasses somehow managed to stay on, but only just. Before the stars could clear from my eyes, Mom was already careening full throttle into her rampage about my (poorly) hidden habit. I couldn't tell you exactly what she said, nor is it important. Words in situations like that are superfluous. Her eyes told the story. Anger, frustration, failure, regret, shame, and anxiety all ran one after another in her eyes. I know because I was feeling the exact same way. I think that my parents always had some shame regarding their drinking. We weren't really allowed to acknowledge it growing up and they would freak out whenever the missionaries came to visit. *Hide everything. Show nothing. They don't need to see that.* Only now, we couldn't hide the fact that alcoholism had just become a family tradition. It is a devastating feeling when you understand that you are an addict.

I was confused, worried, scared. What do kids usually do when they get scared? Go to their parents? Well, mine had just belted me in the chops and was speeding off to the church to do some last-minute cleaning. I didn't have any other option. I sped off to follow her.

I got to the church shortly after Mom did, but I stayed in my car to finish my cigarette. My trembling hand kept knocking the ashes into my lap. My adrenaline was still pumping from my mom's slap. I knew that I had a problem, but I didn't know what to say. Alcoholism was never acknowledged in the house, so asking for help was absolutely unfamiliar territory. *Still*, I thought, *there must be some sort of motherly instinct that enables her to see through all this shit. There has to be some higher design there that will help to put aside all that.* I needed help and I knew it. I stamped out my smoke and walked inside.

The halls were silent and dark. The pictures and awards on the wall of fame sparkled in the waning sun. The smiles of the current crop of good Mormon boys bore into me, knowing my reason for walking the halls. I broke away from them and went deeper in. I ran my fingers across the corrugated walls, reacquainting myself with their rough, unpleasant texture. I passed the seminary classroom where I had first learned the Word of Wisdom before falling asleep and dreaming of Ms. Overbite and the disembodied head of Mr. Fluffums.

Those days had turned to ghosts. Now they whispered to me, skating across the icy fear that every addict who has been found out knows. I turned the corner, past the Primary classroom where I sang 'Popcorn Popping on the Apricot Tree' and 'I Hope They Call Me on a Mission'. The faint melody played in my head as I walked toward the only open door in the church—the library.

Mom was inside, shuffling old copies of the Ensign around and rearranging the art supplies.

I cleared my throat. "Mom?"

She spun around, surprised. "What the hell are you doing here?"

I shrugged. I could feel my head burning. "I need help."

"Just go home. Get out of here. I don't have anything to say to you," she finished as she slammed a hymnal into a cabinet.

"I need help, Mom. I'm asking you for help," I said meekly.

She shook her head. "Do what you want. You're grown."

I was becoming more distressed. I wanted to…I don't know. I don't know what I hoped to accomplish or what I expected. Looking back on the situation, I know now that she could never give me the help that I needed, nor could my father. You can't help others if you won't help yourself first. An active alcoholic reaching out to an active alcoholic for help? That ain't happening. It felt like my mom had given up on me, but through time, I now see that she was just scared for her boy. I can understand that now, but at the time…

"Fuck it," I said and fell back into the darkness of the hallway. I wanted to get the fuck out of there as quickly as possible. I remembered that I could cut through the chapel and get to the other side of the church, so I did. I flipped on the lights and they hummed to life. The chairs were stacked neatly along the walls, waiting for Sunday. The piano was silent. The pulpit was bare. I took a deep breath and shut my eyes. I let the silence and emptiness of that room fill me. The last thing I saw in that room before I flipped off the light was a hymnal with the cover torn off sitting on top of an unused organ. Just another empty room.

It wasn't long after that I left home for good. I wanted to rejoin the living and I needed to be sober to do so. There was no way to get sober in that house. I packed up my possessions and moved into a shit-box apartment on the north side of Youngstown. Now, when I say shit-box apartment, I'm not being hyperbolic. It was a *literal shit-box*. There was petrified dog shit and dried animal piss all over the floors and walls. It wasn't exactly what I had in mind, but that's what 50 bucks a month gets you. I spent the first month of my sobriety cleaning that place to make it habitable. There was no heat or adequate insulation, so my coat and gloves stayed on through the winter. Every night, my girlfriend and I would play *'Gunshots or Fireworks'*, a ghetto favorite. Every night, I faced the urge to drink. Every night, I somehow made it through.

I started seeing a therapist around this time and began the process of reinvention. Well, not reinvention. Maybe reclamation is a better word. I had to reclaim my life. I had to learn about myself, who I was, what I was capable of, and most importantly, what I would do with that knowledge. What choice would I make every day? Would I choose to be the person I was yesterday, or be the man I am today? I made that choice every night until I had 30 days sober. 30 days turned to 60 days, and 60 days turned to 90 days. I started passing my classes again. 90 to 180 days. I made the Dean's list. 180 to 365. *A year.* All that time because of a simple choice. *To be or not to be.*

At the time of this writing, I have 13 years sober. *Lucky 13!* In reality, I only have what I do today. Yesterday was fun, but it doesn't make me sober today. Each day, I get up and make the choice to reclaim my life. When I made the choice to get sober 13 years ago, one of the ways that I reclaimed my life was by resigning from the church and taking ownership of my destiny. If I were going to live life in my own way, independent of the choices of my family and their own issues, that meant finally acknowledging that the link between myself and the church was one that I did not want. For some, leaving the church (like leaving an addiction) is a terrifying prospect. We want to stay in the addiction because we know it. We may not feel great while we are in it, but drugs (like church) make us not care how shitty we feel. You trade in feeling good for feeling less bad. In both instances, what I gained by leaving those old ways behind was…myself.

Chapter 13

Pascal's Wager (or It Don't Make No Goddamn Sense!)

The best way to become an atheist is to study religion. There is no better way to the path of rationality. It's kinda like shining a flashlight under your bed or in your closet when you are a child. When you turn the lights on, you see that there is no boogeyman and you can sleep better. The more light you shine on religion, the less it makes sense. It's liberating.

In college, I minored in religion. I figured that a degree in English made me *pretty much* unemployable and I wanted to go the extra step and make myself *completely* unemployable. Plus, coming from a religion as strict and mysterious as Mormonism kinda helped me write papers. Teachers love that shit. Whenever I'd explain my background, I would get all the same questions about polygamy, prophecy, and *"why no coffee?"* This time, I answered all the questions straight—no bullshit. I was done with childish games.

Anyway, while I was in college, I started looking into the history of the church and learning things that, well, don't make the church look too good. I read about Joseph Smith's polygamy and his penchant for marrying women who were already married. I read about how he had taken child brides and used threats of eternal damnation in order to coerce their family into allowing it. I read about his attempt to destroy a press that was ready to publish an exposé of his misdeeds and how that led to him being arrested and eventually killed. I won't say that he was martyred because I don't believe that he was killed for what he believed. I think he was killed because he fucked up and people had enough of his polygamy and minor league terrorism. I won't bother going into detail about it because there are better books by better authors that cover the subject. Do yourself a favor, read the CES Letter. It's fascinating and free.

I read all this with fresh eyes. I had never known this about the church. Information like this was labeled "Anti-Mormon" as was the DNA and archeological evidence that disproved the Book of Mormon. This stuff was kept out of our reach while in the church. We were told, "Down that path lies deception, Satan, and sadness." In other words, it was kept in the dark. It became the boogeyman. They *liked* their boogeyman. In a sense, every religion has their boogeyman that they can call on in order to keep the people in line. All it takes is for someone to shine a little light...

The more I read, the brighter it got. I felt physically ill thinking that my name, my life was tied to this thing. I was in line with pedophiles, charlatans, racists, liars, and adulterers. And that was just Joseph Smith. Brigham Young's racism, the Mountain Meadows massacre, and the revelation of the 'second anointing' ceremonies further cemented my desire to sever my relationship with the church. Still, I didn't know what to do with this information. Was it possible to get away from this? Was it like a street gang or the Catholic church; blood in, blood out? The more I thought about this conflict taking place inside, the more these old memories popped in. That's when I remembered an incident from my youth tied to a word that I had stumbled across: apostate.

The first time I heard the term 'apostate' was when I was 14 years old. There was a kid who went to our church for a few months who was not well-liked by anyone in the congregation. He was loud, brash, arrogant, and devilishly handsome. Normally, Crack Rock Johnny and myself would have probably recruited him to be in our band. However, even the mighty Crack Rock Johnny wouldn't touch him. It was rumored that he was a gay apostate and that he was trying to recruit all the young men and women into his cult of gay apostasy. No joke, it was like the Mormon version of Satanic Panic. Now, looking back on it, the Cult of Gay Apostasy sounds like it would be a pretty good time, almost like a mix between Rocky Horror and Hedwig and the Angry Inch.

Anyway, one Sunday, Johnny rushed up to me in the hall, pointed this kid out, and uttered the word 'apostate' alongside some other choice words.

"Apostate? What does that mean?" I asked with intense curiosity. Whatever it was, it must be really bad. I'd never seen Johnny this scared, and I once saw him piss on a cop car with the cop still inside. I mean, if Johnny was scared of it, this must be some serious shit!

"It means he doesn't believe Joseph Smith was the prophet!" he said. "He thinks that he made up the Book of Mormon! It's fucked up, right?" I nodded in agreement. I knew better than to stop Johnny when he was on a roll. I watched the accused apostate march through the hallway with his head held high, an odd calm around him.

As a Mormon, you are taught that those who question the validity of the claims of the prophet are not to be associated with. Mormonism, like all demanding religions, regulates the information that the members can access. It's how you keep the devoted from pulling back the curtain. This kid was probably the first 'apostate' that ever got through the doors. Needless to say, he didn't stick around. Rumor had it that the Elders came by the family's house and "suggested" that they take some time to "reevaluate their position in the church". Basically, they told them to *fuck the fuck off*. I thought about this kid and his quiet confidence in the face of all that hatred and fear. I tumbled that rough word 'apostate' in my head till it became smooth. *It's just a word.*

Not long after that, I stumbled across an online community of Ex-Mormons, something that I had no idea even existed. It was a moment when I remember feeling that my world had just expanded. Reading through the individual stories, hearing the experiences from people who had left the church, what it meant to them, how they lost family, how they found themselves, all of it overwhelmed me. It also put my experience into perspective. I had it better than most. Women shared stories of being tethered to a family and a marriage that they had no choice in. LGBT people told horror stories about conversion therapies where they were tortured while watching pornography. Men and women both told stories of losing their children and parents after leaving the church. If a church can do this to their members, how can it be 'true'? My heart broke for these people. I never wanted this to happen to anyone else, if

I could help it. That's when I saw the tiny tab that read 'resignation'. I clicked it, wondering what it meant. I read post after post about how people resigned from the church, severed their association with this organization that they had been so hurt by. Testimonies of freedom, happiness, peace of mind, and endless possibilities scrolled by. It was inspiring. I had no idea that you could resign.

Still, I wondered if I would have the guts to do it. What would my family say? How would I feel after it? I kicked it around for a while. Even though I didn't believe in God and hadn't gone to church for a long time, it's still an issue that the family might get iffy about. Then again, I had already severed (for the most part) the relationship that I used to have with my family when I stopped drinking. I had, in a sense, already left a religion; the religion of alcoholism. How much more strained could my relationship with my family be? *Why bother being part of a club that I don't want to belong to? Shit,* I thought, *let's roll these bones and see what the fuck happens!* I sent my resignation letter to Salt Lake City the next day.

Now, in preparation, I read the stories from the individuals who had resigned and what I might expect to feel or experience after resignation. Some people felt overwhelming joy, some felt existential dread, some felt the urge to try to get their loved ones to follow suit. I'll tell you the truth, I felt none of that. It was almost like cancelling a magazine subscription. I was glad that I didn't have to pay for something I don't read. That was how I initially felt. I was done with it, and as far as I was concerned, it was done with me. However, the church wasn't exactly done with me.

I had seen that individuals who resigned did experience some harassment from church members and officials regarding their resignation. Almost all of them had some kind of story about Bishops, missionaries, old church friends, or someone reaching out to them and their extended families, trying to get them to come back to church. In some cases, this pressure led to some dire consequences. I had assumed that there might be one or two people who would reach out to my family, so I decided that I would break the news myself and head off any kind of church intervention. I took the drive out to my parent's house, passing many of the monuments that I would on any dreadful Sunday. These markers no longer held any dread in them for me. The tie had been severed. All that was left was the glorious waning summer sun.

I met my mom in the living room and told her about my resignation. She had been Mormon only in name really, so there wasn't any real dread or consequence. Her response was simple, direct.

"Well, as long as you still believe in something."

"Of course," I said. "I believe in me. I believe in you. I believe in people."

"Well, you be careful believing in people," she said. "You'll get your ass screwed for that if you're not careful." My mom always had a way with words. My relationship with my parents had gotten a bit better after there was some space between us. Sobriety forces you to be kinder to others, especially if they are going through the same thing you did. I started seeing my parents more as people rather than parents. In short, I grew up. I finished my coffee and headed outside to where my dad was busy filling in holes in the yard. For some reason, there were always holes in our yard. I could never figure it out. We didn't have gophers or moles. Maybe it was some guy searching for buried treasure or an old stash of trucker porn, I dunno. All I know is that Dad was out there every summer, a wheelbarrow full of rocks, filling in holes.

As I've stated in earlier stories, my father is a man of few words—three to be exact. Those words are *yep, nope,* and *shit.* Only on a few occasions has he reached into his subconscious and found different words for a needed situation. I didn't expect that this situation would require more than his usual three words. I expected a short exchange of possibly one, maybe two words at most. Expectations, however, can be subverted from time to time.

He shook a shovelful of rocks into a particularly large hole and stubbed out his cigarette into an empty Natural Light can, looked up, and nodded. He lit up another cigarette and went back to work.

"Hey, Dad. Got some more holes to fill in?" I said, trying to make conversation.

"Yep," he replied.

"Awesome," I replied, lighting my own cigarette.

"Nope," he said as he stamped down another shovelful into the hole.

I watched the dragonflies chase one another around the yard, wondering how to break it to Dad. *How do I approach this? Just blurt it out? Mom didn't seem to care, so I don't think he will either.* I didn't know how long to keep the conversation going before I broke the news to him. My dad is a hard man to read. I'm sure that he's had emotions in his life; it's just that I've never seen them. It makes sense why he played things so close to his chest. Men—especially men in an environment like the one my dad grew up in—aren't allowed to show emotions. It's about self-preservation. If anyone was going to make the move, it had to be me.

"Ah, fuck it," I said as I tossed my cigarette out into the yard. "Dad, I resigned from the church, so don't be surprised if you get a call from the bishop or someone. You mind if I bum a smoke?"

Dad parked his shovel next to the hole that he was working on, gave me a quizzical look, and handed me his pack of cigarettes. He watched me as I lit one and handed him the pack. "What does that mean?" he asked.

I was astounded. This was way beyond his yearly quota for word expenditure. Plus, he seemed like he really wanted to know. This was uncharted territory for me. *Jesus, might I actually get a conversation out of this man?*

"Um," I started. "Well, it means that I sent in my resignation letter, taking my name out of the church, off the records, off the phone list and whatever else they got on me. It's honestly been a long time coming. I haven't been attending since I was like 16, I haven't believed since I was 12, and I really don't want to have my name associated with a church that treats gays and women like they do." I could see that he was taking in my words with sincerity. "It's not something that I take lightly, Dad," I reassured him. "I can't morally have my name attached to something like that."

Dad lit up another cigarette and watched the tip glow. Something was rolling around in his head, but I didn't know what. In my entire life, I had only seen Dad at church *maybe* five times. Whenever the missionaries or home teachers came over, he would always be outside fixing his car or clipping the trees or in bed. I had *never* seen him take a calling in the church, pay tithing, accept sacrament, or even pray at Thanksgiving dinner. I had always assumed that religion or spirituality was never, ever a factor in his life. It was curious that he seemed to be thinking about what I said with such intensity. What was going to be his response?

He took a long drag on his cigarette. "You know I never went to church like you guys did," he said through a thick cloud of smoke. "I never really followed it that much either." He dragged on his cigarette again. "But that doesn't mean I don't *believe* it."

"Yeah?" I asked. His sincerity was astounding. He had never talked about the church before. "I appreciate that, Dad. I'm not saying that it's wrong to believe. I'm just saying that *I* don't believe it. I got no beef with anyone that wants to go to church or the temple. It's just…leave me out of it, that's all."

He nodded and stamped out his cigarette. "What if you're wrong?"

"I'm sorry?"

"What if you're wrong?" he asked again. "For me, I kinda see it as…insurance. You know how you got insurance on your car in case something happens?"

"Yeah, of course."

"Nobody plans on getting in an accident, but if they do, they got their ass covered. That's how I see church. It's like, if I die and I don't got a church, I might go to hell. It's better to be safe than sorry."

I nodded. I could see his point of view. He was not a religious man. He lived by his own code. However, like most people, I think he needed that safety net. It's the reason that a lot of people stay inactive, like he did, rather than resign from the Mormon church. It's like an insurance policy. It is a lot easier to answer to God why you haven't been to church vs. why you denounced the church. Having my own son, I can now understand better his concern for my "soul". Fathers are tricky creatures. We want our sons to be their own men, providing that they are being safe about it. Most of us have yet to learn how to express this emotionally, so we falter with our words. I don't think he thought too much on God, I think that he just didn't want to end up back in hell.

At the time, I didn't know it, but my dad was arguing Pascal's Wager. For those of you cool cats and kittens who don't know, Pascal's Wager is named after Blaise Pascal, a 17th century French Philosopher. The basic idea is that humans bet with their lives that God exists or does not exist. If you bet that there is a God and it turns out there wasn't one, you don't lose anything. If you bet that there is no God and you lose, you are dammed for all eternity. So, according to this, it's *safer to bet that God exists*. It's an afterlife insurance policy, brought to you by the insurance offices of Smith, Young, and Monson. Solid logic, right?

Well, turns out there are several huge problems with Pascal's Wager, the biggest of which is that there is *more than one religion that professes to be true*. Each of the big three monotheistic religions (Islam, Judaism, and Christianity) professes to be the one true religion of God. Now, looking at only the Christian religion, there are about 33,000 different denominations, all of which profess to be the true (or preferred) version of Christianity. *Mormonism is one of 33,000.* Now, those are big numbers to plug into Pascal's Wager. Not only would we have to pick the correct monotheist religion (Islam, Christianity, or Judaism), we would also have to pick the correct denomination of that religion. For instance, if the Mormon God is the real God and you happen to be Catholic, you won't be able to get into the Celestial Kingdom because you haven't done the temple work on Earth. Now, suppose Islam is the correct religion. If you grew up eating bacon and pork rinds every Sunday, your ass ain't getting near Allah. So, it becomes less about believing in God, but *which* God, then figuring out *which version* of that one God to go with. *But wait, there's more!*

What about polytheists? I mean, suppose that Thor and Odin are the ones who call the shots in the afterlife. Am I not going to get to go to Valhalla because I haven't died bravely on the glorious field of battle? Should I start a war? Well, since I'm an American, I suppose I could just wait for the next one to start. Why not take people who believe in the Greek and Roman gods seriously? They have just as much proof that their Gods exist as any other church does. Plus, you get to drink wine and wear togas. *Viva l'Italia!*

Another issue I have with Pascal's Wager is that belief, not action, seems to be the key factor in reaping the rewards of heaven. That assumption just doesn't sit right with me. Let's say that there is someone who is living life in accordance with some objective moral good. They are nice to people, helpful, genuine, and earnestly try to make the world a better place. They live a life of service to others. What if the only difference between them and a theist who also lives a life of service is that they don't believe in God? In this equation, God would throw the non-believer in hell while the other goes to heaven. He would do so, not based on their actions, but on whether or not they believed something that they could not see. Meanwhile, murderers on death row can repent at the end of their lives and be "saved" by Christ the Redeemer. It seems that God is a little more concerned with appearances than intention. Now, a God like that is someone that is hardly worth worshipping.

Also, let's talk about being righteous for righteousness sake. One should *want* to act good toward one's fellow person *as its own reward*, not out of some fear of hell. If the only reason that you don't rape and murder is because it is against God's law (which it really isn't, BTW), then that means your internal morality is nonexistent. If you need God to tell you that it's wrong to kill and rape, you need to do some serious work on yourself. If you need some concrete examples of religious people raping and murdering while still professing belief in God, look at the conflict in Northern Ireland, the sexual abuse history of the Catholic Church, the Mountain Meadows Massacre, and the Branch Davidian cult in Waco Texas.

After our discussion, I think I understood my dad a bit better, at least on the subject of spirituality. When you become an adult, it is important that you see your parents as human beings. It allows you to forgive them and also to understand their strengths better. It also allows you to take control of your own decisions more and to be appreciative of them. When I got sober, my relationship with my family changed. We still don't discuss it, the same way we don't discuss religion. That's fine. Nowadays, I don't need to discuss that stuff with them. *I just end up writing books about it.*

Chapter 14

Why Are You So Angry? (or You Can Leave it, But You Can't Leave it Alone)

Shortly after I had "the talk" with my parents, a few "well-meaning" members reached out to me to "voice their concerns" and to try to bring me "back to the fold." What was curious was that some of these people I had never met before. It's rather hard to take someone's threat of "an eternity in outer darkness" seriously when I've never met the guy before. However, I resisted the urge to tell them to shove it up their ass. That kind of talk only makes these people more entrenched, and that's not what I wanted at all. The one thing that I wanted, I never got. What was that, you ask? I wanted an honest, open discussion about church history, church doctrine, and the notion of God. However, all I got was the canned responses, telling me that I've been "led astray" and that "sin only seems fun". I politely declined their invitation to "pray on it" and stated that, while I don't agree with their religion, I would be more than happy to keep in contact with them as friends and colleagues. Needless to say, they didn't take me up on that offer. What they did instead was to label me an apostate and my writings as 'anti-Mormon'. *See, kids, kindness gets you nowhere.* Ex-Mormons carry a stigma, even among our own families. When you leave the church, it's both said and unsaid that you are now an outsider. It can get lonely. That's the price of freedom, I guess.

So, in true nitpicking asshole fashion, I am going to address some of the statements and assumptions that Mormons have about people who leave the church. These are things that Ex-Mormons hear ad nauseam when one leaves the church. Let's start with the most popular phrase that we hear:

You can leave the church, but you can't leave it alone.

Before we get into this one, I'll pose this question: Did you ever have a sore in your mouth (that you may or may not have gotten from a less than faithful ex-girlfriend?). It's in your mouth, it hurts, but yet you keep on poking at it with your tongue, don't you? This is the image that a lot of people in the church get of Ex-Mormons. Supposedly, we are miserable because we keep poking at our mouth sores. This phrase 'you can leave it, but you can't leave it alone' implies that if we as Ex-Mormons are indeed as happy as we say we are, there should be no reason for us to shit on someone else's religion. Now, to be fair, I have to say that I personally have no bones with anyone who wants to be Mormon. That's cool. This is America where you can buy a gun and a cheeseburger within 20 feet of one another, so we should have no issues with religious freedom. You do you. In fact, I am so comfortable with others being Mormon that never have I once ever called someone or came to someone's door trying to get them to be an Ex-Mormon with me. I wish the people in the church extended me the same courtesy.

No, my issue with the church comes from the church's history of hiding information from its members, including the number and ages of the wives of Joseph Smith and Brigham Young. I also have an issue with the fact that they will simultaneously hide this information from their members or discourage them from researching it, but will gladly take 10% of their money with no issue. *Apparently, in the kingdom of heaven, money talks and bullshit walks.* That's why I find it hard to leave the church alone. Let me put it to you this way—if you are driving down the road and you pass a hazardous object in the opposite lane, it is courteous and potentially life-saving to warn other drivers about it by flashing your lights. Whether or not they choose to heed your warning is on them, but you did what was *morally* right. That is how I feel about 'not leaving the church alone'. You don't have to listen to what I have to say, but that does not change the moral obligation that *I* have to make sure that you have all the information to make an accurate judgment about the church. I'm giving you the benefit of information, whereas the church wouldn't even do *that* for you.

Another assumption that many Mormons make about Ex-Mormons is that we left because we were "offended". The conversation usually sounds something like this:

> **Sister 1:** Did you hear that Jeffrey left the church?
>
> **Sister 2:** Oh gosh! Why, oh why would he do that?
>
> **Sister 1:** I don't know. I bet it was the talk that the bishop gave about not having facial hair.
>
> **Sister 2:** That makes sense! He's been trying to grow his beard out for a month instead of focusing on his mission!

Sounds stupid, right? Well…it is. Ex-Mormons don't leave for petty shit like that. Most people leave the church because they read about church history. They leave because of the *facts*. For instance, the fact that there is no archeological or DNA evidence supporting the claims of the Book of Mormon. Or the fact that Joseph Smith had multiple wives, one of which was as young as 14 years old. Or the fact that until 1978, African-Americans were not allowed to hold priesthood offices in the church. Or the fact that the Book of Abraham was a fabrication. *So many facts!* Stating that we are offended downplays a very serious and Earth-shattering crisis of faith that some never recover from. By painting Ex-Mormons as flakes, it's a way the church keeps its followers in line. Simple.

My favorite one that I heard when I left was that I've "intellectualized myself out of a testimony," which essentially means that I got too smart for my own good. This took place not long after I left the church, from an old priesthood leader who was also a Scoutmaster. For the purposes of this story, let's call him Brother Faith because logic waved bye-bye to this guy a long time ago. Now, I am not a smart man. Anyone who sniffed as much glue as I did in high school was not going to end up on the honor roll. But even a simpleton such as myself could see through what the church (and this guy) tried to pass off as *fact*. I am going to be quoting directly from the exchange that happened:

> *"I fear for now though you have intellectualized yourself out of a testimony of the Savior and His divine role in life. You indicate*

you love His teachings and as a result I assume you try to live by them, but what you fail to allow yourself to comprehend for now is that He was so much more than a teacher. I won't preach on this, but someday after your readings and research I hope you try to put the "facts" aside and let faith find a place in your life.

"We had a guy out here leave the church because DNA testing on the American Indians, who the Book of Mormon say are descendants of the literal house of Israel through Lehi, does not match the DNA of today's Jews who populate Israel. I laugh at such preposterous testing because do people actually think God would make it that easy!? If we have fact where does that leave faith?

"Elder Neal A. Maxwell said it best: 'Science will not be able to prove or disprove holy writ, however enough plausible evidence will come forth to prevent the scoffers from having a field day, but not enough to prevent the

243

requirement of faith'. It all comes down to faith, my friend."

The line that stuck out to me is "If we have fact, where does that leave faith?" I mean, isn't that the quintessential argument for all religions? The bitter truth about faith is that it makes you feel good. Faith is childlike—it's simple. *The world makes sense with faith.* If something bad happens to you, it is easier to say, "It's all part of God's plan," than to say, "Maybe bad stuff happens for no reason." This is something that I learned when I was very young, in a very profound way. When I was about eight years old, shortly after I was baptized, my Oma got cancer. We visited her in the hospital, kept her comfy at home, did everything that we could do physically and medically for her. My mom and everyone at church told me that it wasn't enough, though. It was important that I also prayed every day. I had to pray every day to make sure that God knew how important Oma was to me. So, I prayed every day. I prayed in English, in German, and I made up a special prayer just for Oma. I did this for a long time to help my Oma get better. She did not. She died. Had I done something wrong? Did I not pray hard enough? Did I say the wrong words? I didn't know, but I felt extraordinarily guilty for my Oma's death.

Of course, I never told anyone this. Death wasn't (and still isn't) discussed freely within my family. No one at the church bothered to let me know that sometimes nature is more powerful than prayer. Sometimes cancer is more powerful than human will. Sometimes bad things happen to good people for no reason. Sometimes people die and there is nothing that you can do. After that, my prayers more or less became meaningless incantations used to placate my mom and the church. Empty words. I figured if God didn't want to help Oma beat cancer, he probably didn't care too much about anything else I had to say. It's hard to have faith after something like that.

Church *was* and *is* a giant game of make-believe played primarily by adults. They make-believe that some competent being is in control of their destiny. They make-believe that life is a fight between good and evil. Most of all, they make-believe that they are all headed to someplace easier and better than this. They live their lives expecting a reward when they are blind to the fact that *life itself* is the reward. Being aware of our own mortality can be either a blessing or a curse. If you live as if you are not in control of your own destiny, that you are meant to please some deity, then life is going to be terrifying. However, if you accept your fate as a mortal being, someone who has a limited time in which to experience life, then why not take full advantage and credit for it? In the end, we are the masters of our destiny, answerable only to ourselves. If we do need to have faith, it should not be placed in God, but in *ourselves*.

In the Mormon religion, Outer Darkness is a place where people who reject the teaching of the church go to live out their eternity. It is not hell. There is no fire, no brimstone, no torture, no Satan. Evil people do not go there. It is reserved only for those who hear the gospel and refuse to accept it. The term Outer Darkness comes from the idea that it is not the torture that inflicts pain, but being away from the light of God that is torture. It is the lack of contact, warmth, love, happiness, and joy that tortures you. That is why

Mormons so desperately want to avoid Outer Darkness. The irony is that many of us Ex-Mormons feel that lack of connection, warmth, love, and joy while we are still members. Outer Darkness becomes an isolation of thought and conscience. We feel disconnected from the light within ourselves, the true definition of divinity. It's ironic that the steps that are meant to keep you out of Outer Darkness can push you deeper into it.

In conclusion, I will say this: the anger that Ex-Mormons feel is valid. We've put so much time, effort, and money into an organization that demands so much. It demands obedience, resistance to natural questions, and creates a complex in us that causes us to second-guess science and factual history. The reason we can't leave it alone is because *it refuses to leave us alone*. Our thoughts, our feelings, our life is tainted by this system of rigorous thought control. Our families and our communities are linked to the church. We are demonized for asking questions that require actual answers. Finally, we can't leave it alone because the people that we love and care about might still be there.

I've been out of the church now for close to 13 years. In that time, I have studied religion, talked with people from all over the world, from every race, and every creed. I have been demonized for being an atheist, commended for being compassionate, worked with addicts, homeless people, and tried to be of service wherever I could. By leaving the constraints of religion, I've been able to explore my own life in a much more honest and open manner. In leaving the church, I was able to define a healthy boundary between myself and those in my family. By being honest with myself, I have been able to help others to be honest with themselves. Finally, in my time away from the church, I've found something worth having faith in—people.

Outer Darkness

"Being a Humanist means trying to behave decently without expectation of rewards or punishment after you are dead."

— *Kurt Vonnegut*

"Religion is like a pair of shoes...Find one that fits for you, but don't make me wear your shoes."

— *George Carlin*

TALES FROM OUTER DARKNESS

Epilogue

To Outer Darkness and Beyond!

My family and I go to the zoo frequently. Los Angeles has a fine zoo and the membership fees are pretty reasonable. Plus, little kids love looking at animals. My son is enamored with flamingos and elephants. Every time he sees the flamingo exhibit, he loses his shit. I stand back and watch him with his mother, excitedly pointing out the flamingos. Pretty soon, he'll be old enough to watch *Jurassic Park* and then his dinosaur phase will start in earnest. In a way, I think the reason that children identify so much with animals is because they have so much in common with them. They know very little of social cues, run predominantly on instinct, and piss and shit wherever they please, at least till they get a little older.

We recently went to the zoo to shake the quarantine out of our hair and to get some much-needed fresh air (or as fresh as you can get in Los Angeles). I was busy checking the score of the Dodgers game when I felt a tap on my shoulder. I looked up to see my wife giving me a wicked little smile.

"Yes, my dear?" I answered, looking for the punchline. I knew that she had something up her sleeve.

"They found you!" she said playfully.

I let out a cartoonish gasp that sent my son into hysterics. "Who's found me this time?"

"Your people!" she responded, pointing behind me.

I turned to see a group of five missionaries, all white and delightsome, excitedly making their way into the zoo. The playful smile faded from my face and I focused on my boy who was chewing on a leaf.

My people.

I always get nervous when I see missionaries. Individually, they are just normal 18-year-old kids who are experiencing the world for the first time. Idealistic, energetic, positive-minded young men and women who earnestly think that they can change the world. *Why be nervous around that?*

Part of the nervousness comes from seeing the physical salesmen of the church that I left behind. For a brief moment, it does feel like they've been after you. Of course, that's ridiculous, but for a second, it isn't. Another part of the nervousness I have is that my wife will want to talk to them. I told her about all the beliefs and practices, which for a Catholic is hilarious. She wants to know more about "Macaroni" and "Moron" and "Joseph Smith and the Amazing Technicolor Golden Plates". One day, I'll unleash her on some poor kid from Utah, but not at the zoo.

What makes me the most nervous when I see missionaries out and about is that I remember what they said about people who left the church. I remember the disgust and fear as they told stories about apostates becoming instantly addicted to heroin and hookers the day they left the church. I remember the stories they told to us kids about Outer Darkness.

Outer Darkness is a term used by the Mormons to describe what happens to people who don't accept the teachings of the church. The best way to describe it would be as a sort of passive hell. There is no fire, no

Satan, no torture, no Hitler, just nothing. It is so-called because the souls who are banished there are away from the light of God. Now, the thought behind it is that being away from the light of God is worse than any suffering that hell could bring you, that being away from your family and loved ones for all eternity is a just punishment for not accepting the gospel. Most Christian denominations have a version of punishment for not believing, so it's nothing new. I heard about this concept from an early age, just like my Catholic and Protestant friends heard about hell. God loves us so much that he would ensure your constant misery for all eternity because you didn't believe in him based on no evidence. Seems legit.

The thing about missionaries is this: when I look at their bright faces, I know that, one day, they will have to come across someone like me. That person will tell their story. The light will go out of the face of that missionary. They will tell the non-believer to pray on it. They will warn them of the consequences of not returning to the church. They might even reach out to the non-believer's family to interfere. That non-believer will become another warning tale to the next batch of Mormon youth. Not a person, but a warning. I suppose that's why I avoid the missionaries—I don't want to be reduced to a warning. At least not at the zoo.

I also think that I get nervous when I see missionaries because I don't want them trying to sell their church to my son. As a parent, you have this primal mission to protect your child from all threats, physical and intellectual. The Mormon church doesn't pose any physical threat to me and my family, but it most certainly poses an intellectual one. Any church that places a limitation on what kinds of questions they can ask is an intellectual threat. Any church that tells children that they can't love who they want to love is an intellectual threat. Any church that tells children that their family members who don't follow the teaching of the church are unrighteous is an intellectual threat. I can't have that around my boy.

However, we reach a conundrum. If I keep him away from all influence of religion, doesn't that make me just as bad as a high-demand church? Doesn't that make me guilty of intellectual censorship? I think it could. So, what's to be done?

Parenting has no easy answers. You do the best you can and hope the kid can find a good shrink. I think raising someone with a healthy degree of skepticism is important, especially in the world we live in. We have political misinformation, anti-vax conspiracy theorists, flat-earth nutjobs, and a host of other intellectual terrorists that prey on the weak-minded and those who can't engage in critical thinking. George Carlin once said, "It's not important to get your kids to read. It's important to get your kids to question what they read."

I can't shield the world from my boy, nor would I want to. He needs to see and experience what he will. What I can do is *try* to get him to question it. He will see a thousand different religions. He'll hear legends from countries all over the world. He's going to meet communists, right-wingers, Democrats, Republicans, political dissidents. He needs to be able to explore these ideologies and not allow them to reduce him to a label on a t-shirt. With any luck, he will be fully immersed in this world, but be able to stay afloat. Or maybe he'll join the Mormon church, or become a Catholic, or become a Buddhist. Ultimately, it's not up to me. He has to live his life *his* way. In the end, we all have to answer to ourselves.

I suppose that, in a small way, that is why I sat down to write these experiences out. I obviously didn't write it for the money, though if I make a buck or two, I wouldn't mind that. *Those gambling addictions and secret families won't pay for themselves!* Ultimately, I had to explore the experiences of being part of, and leaving a church that is as demanding as the Mormon church. It was necessary for me, not only as a parent, but as a living, learning adult, to come to peace with these experiences. Maybe by doing this, I show my boy how to explore his feelings, rather than drink them away like I did. With any luck, I carry on the tradition that my parents started, which is doing better than *their* parents did. Maybe some of you in the Mormon church who are reading this might gain an understanding of what it was like to be a weird kid in the church. Maybe you will start to take it easy on the weird kids. For those who are questioning their path, perhaps this book offers some perspective and illumination on the Mormon church and the effects religion has on the minds of young people.

I've gotten to a point in my life where the things that scared me as a kid don't scare me anymore. I used to be terrified of ghosts and demons and monsters, especially the ones I'd see on MonsterVision. Most of all, I was afraid of the dark. As an adult, I'm not afraid of ghosts or demons or monsters, but rather what those ideas represent. The idea that life might be meaningless and brief is depressing. The idea that sometimes evil happens with no reason is agonizing. However, these are also perfect adverts for why we shouldn't be scared. Being afraid of the finality and futility of life doesn't make any sense. We don't have time for that. The only thing, really, that we have is each other, and even then, it's only for a little bit. Why spend that time fixated on an afterlife that might not be there? Why stress about living by someone else's rules? Why spend your life dodging ghosts and demons and monsters? Most of all, why be afraid of the dark?

Shameless Plug!

Hey there, you lovely reader! Got a second? I wanna say thanks for reading my book. Regardless if you loved it or hated it, or maybe fell somewhere in the middle, I appreciate the time you gave to read this. If you have a little more time, I would really appreciate a review on Amazon. If you liked it, give it a review! If you hated it, give it a review! If you think that I am a hack-fraud who doesn't know the first thing about writing, give it a review! Once again, thanks and all my best.

About the Author

Alan Young is a novelist, blogger, and screenwriter, who has a love for sci-fi, horror, fantasy, and most of all, quirky and unusual characters. His clever, ironic, and heartwarming stories explore characters facing spectacular forces while having to navigate their everyday lives.

He has also written extensively about his transition out of the Church of Jesus Christ of Latter-day Saints and explored the struggles of making meaning out of a secular world. When he is not busy writing, he enjoys watching terrible B-movies with his family in Covina.

Visit alanyoungwriter.wordpress.com to stay up to date on new books, short stories, and to follow his blog!